In *How To Live Life on Purpose*, my dear friend, Art Sepúlveda, accurately depicts the need for the church to break through our own boundaries and move forward into the supernatural. His book will help open the door to an amazing life of passion and adventure.

John Bevere
Author/Speaker
Messenger International
USA/Australia/United Kingdom

Pastor Sepúlveda is truly a man of vision. His desire to see believers go to higher levels of power, wisdom, and success in Christ is not only changing lives in Hawaii, but all over the world as well. Personal change and the ability to make a mark in the world are subjects close to my heart. I am a firm believer that God wants every Christian to break out of the realm of average and tap into the supernatural living outlined in His Word.

Pastor Art Sepúlveda's book, *How To Live Life on Purpose*, helps you to do just that—break out of mediocrity by shattering the ceiling of limitation. Within its pages, you'll learn how to expand your vision, the importance of effective communication and right thinking, and much more. You'll discover how to maximize your potential and fulfill God's purpose for your life. After reading it, nothing will be able to hold you back.

Dr. Creflo A. Dollar
Pastor
World Changers Church International
College Park, Georgia

I am always inspired by people who have the courage to break through barriers to accomplish great things. My friend, Art Sepúlveda, is one of those who has overcome many obstacles and is having an impact in the lives of others. This book contains the principles that will motivate anyone to breakthrough the limitations and containment that have held them back from God's purposes.

Brian Houston
Senior Pastor
Hillsong Church
Sydney, Australia

It is with great joy that I write this endorsement for Pastor Art Sepúlveda's new book, *How To Live Life on Purpose.*

I have known Art and his precious wife, Kuna, for many years, and if there is one thing that I know about both of them, it is this: they are passionate about helping people come into the knowledge of the truth and begin to enjoy the freedom that Jesus shed His blood for.

That's why Art wrote this powerful book. Every page is filled with nuggets of truth that will assist you in learning how to live the way God designed you to live.

I encourage you to read every page with an open mind and an open heart. Regardless of what you may have been told in the past, you can overcome every limitation that has ever attempted to control your life.

It is my prayer that the truth in this book will set you free.

Dr. Jerry Savelle
Jerry Savelle Ministries

HOW TO LIVE
LIFE ON PURPOSE ™

Discover Your Calling
and How You Can Fulfill It

by Art Sepúlveda

Harrison House
Tulsa, Oklahoma

08 07 06 05 04   10 9 8 7 6 5 4 3 2 1

How To Live Life on Purpose™:
Discover Your Calling and How You Can Fulfill It
ISBN 1-57794-321-X
Copyright © 2004 by Art Sepúlveda
550 Queen Street
Honolulu, Hawaii 96813

Published by Harrison House, Inc.
P.O. Box 35035
Tulsa, Oklahoma 74153

Dedication

I dedicate this book to my wife, *Kuna,* the wife of my youth whom God has given to walk with me as my companion on this journey of purpose; and to my children, *Ashley* and *Baby, Nicole, Alexis,* and *Natalie,* upon whom the Hand of God rests and to whom the purpose for their generation is being revealed by the Holy Spirit.

I would also like to dedicate this work to my Mom, *Adeliada Sepúlveda,* without whose persevering belief in me and my pursuit of God's vision, purposes, and calling for my life, this book would never have become a reality.

Loving Husband, Father, and Son
Art Sepúlveda

Acknowledgments

I want to give all the praise and honor to God Almighty, the Creator of heaven and earth through His Son Jesus Christ. He is the revealer of purpose, and I thank Him for providing me the opportunity to hold forth the Word of Life to my generation.

I praise God for blessing me with my wonderful family whom I absolutely love—*Kuna, Ashley* and *Baby, Nicole, Alexis,* and *Natalie.* Words cannot express the joy, fulfillment, honor, pleasure, and rescue they have been to me with their love, gratitude, and genuineness.

I would also like to thank the wonderful congregation of Word of Life Christian Center—our extended family. They have allowed me to pastor them by the gift of the grace of God given to me by the effectual work of His Power.

I am particularly grateful to my pastors, *Pastor César* and *Pastor Claudia Castellanos.* There are not enough words in any language to sufficiently express their value to me, my family, and Word of Life Christian Center.

I'd like to give special thanks to *Pastor Casey Treat, Kenneth* and *Gloria Copeland, Dr. Fredrick K.C.* and *Betty Price, Dr. Jerry Savelle, Jesse Duplantis, Dr. Creflo Dollar, Dave Demola, Brian Houston, Steve Munsey,* and *Bishop Keith* and *Deborah Butler* for their impartation and lives of extraordinary dedication to the Lord. Their uncompromising walks of faith have been tremendous examples that have served to undergird me throughout my years in the ministry.

Finally, I want to give thanks to Candis Chang, Jonell Cockett, and Brent Pharo for their incredible and awesome editorial assistance in the preparation of this book.

Contents

Foreword

How To Live Life on Purpose is written by a true pastor. Art Sepúlveda is committed to communicating practical and powerful truths to you. He wants you to see more, believe more, and live on a higher plane of life. He uses fables, sports, practical parables, and the Bible to help you understand these powerful truths.

Pastor Sepúlveda encourages and empowers you to live life supernaturally, get out of your comfort zone, and go for the best. But he not only exhorts us, he gives us the practical tools to reach that next level. Starting with a vision that is specific, clear, and focused, you will begin to see your future as you *Live Life on Purpose*. You'll learn the eight steps to envisioning your future and seeing it come to pass.

You will see how the Lord has given you a divine helper, the Holy Spirit, to help you see and move into your future. You are not alone; the Holy Spirit is your vision and purpose empowerer. Pastor Art will help you apply these truths to your family, finances, and professional life as you follow "the seven steps to activating the power of vision."

Pastor Sepúlveda will inspire you to speak new words, believe new things, and go for all that life offers you. How you think, talk, and act will be changed by this book. As you journey through this material, it will be exciting to see what change and growth will be manifested in you. LIVE LIFE ON PURPOSE, NOT BY ACCIDENT!

Pastor Casey Treat
Senior Pastor
Christian Faith Center
Seattle, Washington

Introduction

"I cannot believe that the purpose of life is to be 'happy.' I think the purpose of life is to be useful, to be responsible, to be compassionate. It is above all, to matter: to count, to stand for something, to have made some difference that you lived at all."[1]

Leo Calvin Rosten
Passions and Prejudices

As you read this quote, did you go back and read it more than once and ponder its meaning? The first time I read it, deep in my spirit, I felt a big "Yes! That's how I want to be living!" I hope you felt that same excitement and challenge to examine your heart and measure your life against such a goal. That is why I wrote this book—to challenge you to want to live in a manner that counts, that stands for something, that makes some difference that you have lived at all!

Accepting this challenge begins with a *desire* to go beyond where you are now. It requires making a personal decision to move out of your individual comfort zone, existing status quo, or any kind of mediocre mentality that might hold you back. It is only after the fire of your desire is ignited that you will be ready and able to apply the dynamic strategies for living *supernaturally*—above and beyond the ordinary—which I will share with you in the coming chapters.

Supernatural living, as defined in *Webster's New World College Dictionary,* means "existing or occurring outside the normal experience or knowledge of man."[2] It requires a belief in divine intervention. In other words, it takes God. You can't do it on your own or do it your own way.

Unfortunately, people create all sorts of false barriers—or as I like to call them, "glass ceilings"—that keep them from discovering and fulfilling God's purpose in their lives. Because the ceilings are made of glass, they often aren't even aware of the barriers and cannot understand why they matter. As a result, they drift along in life feeling as if they have no purpose or value.

For some, the ceiling drops in place because of how people have defined them. For others, it is because of what Mommy or Daddy did or didn't do when they were children. Then there are those who are hindered by how they think about or see themselves. Real or perceived failures in life may cause them to simply give up trying to move beyond where they are.

When you look at yourself in a mirror, what do you see? What do you say to that reflection looking back at you? Do you like what you see? Would you like to change something about yourself (and not just physical characteristics)? For many of us, it is too uncomfortable to look closely at ourselves in a mirror. However, this exercise is important because you must see yourself clearly before you can go beyond where you are. Many of us don't know what we are or where we are in life and, therefore, we don't know how to move up in life.

In the story of Snow White and the seven dwarfs, the ugly, wicked queen had a magic looking glass into which she would gaze and say, "Mirror, mirror on the wall. Who is the fairest of them all?" She was deceived by her own eyes and saw herself as the most beautiful in the land because that was what she wanted to see. Sometimes we are deceived by what we see in the mirror, either good or bad. We need to see ourselves through the eyes of Jesus, because without seeing and understanding as He does, we have a distorted image of our own lives.

No matter what glass ceilings have been holding you back in life, be assured that you don't have to remain where you are. One thing we know about glass is that it is easily broken. By applying the powerful biblical principles in this book, you can shatter the glass ceilings in your life and live supernaturally by discovering the destiny and purpose to which God has called you.

Moving from where you are to where you want or need to be doesn't happen automatically, but it can happen deliberately in the process of time if you are willing to risk moving out of your holding pattern or neutral normality. Right now, you may have your engine running; you're revving it up, but it is in neutral.

If you have ever driven a stick shift car, you know what it is like to learn to shift gears without grinding them. Care must be taken not to slip a gear and slide back to where you've already been. Likewise, you can't skip gears and expect a smooth ride. Life is also like that. You must move up one level at a time or shift gears in sequence. Learning how to drive a stick shift doesn't happen without making some mistakes along the way. However, the joy of finally sailing down the highway in that little red sports car is worth the initial embarrassment of stalling out on hills and the bucking-bronco effects experienced at intersections.

Mistakes aren't failures, and they are worth the risk. Champion hockey player Wayne Gretzky expressed so well what it means to risk failure in order to gain success when he said, "You miss 100 percent of the shots you never take."[3] You will never make a goal if you don't risk taking some shots at it. If what you have been doing to move out of neutral isn't working, then risk trying something new; and don't be afraid of a few mistakes and bumps along the way.

Now is the time to shift into first gear and start moving slowly until you are ready for the next level God has for you. Many people think there is a great gap between those who live an ordinary life and those who live an extraordinary one. The truth is there is only a fine line between where you are now and the next level. Sometimes all it takes to move up is a small change in your daily habits, a different way of looking at things, or a willingness to get up one more time when you've been knocked down.

Living above and beyond the ordinary is to know that failure isn't fatal, that your faith isn't futile, and that God isn't finished. In reality, the only difference between the ordinary and the extraordinary life is that little extra effort, that little *oomph!* The key is to do what you can do today to come closer to your potential tomorrow.

Where you are now is not all there is, and what you are now is not all God created you to be! Living supernaturally above and beyond the ordinary is knowing what you want, what you are willing to reach for, what price you are willing to pay to push yourself out of your existing comfort zone. It is about finding solutions to get you out of your rut, which is a grave with the ends kicked out! It is about progress, which cannot occur without change, because change is the price you must pay for progress. It is about grasping hold of the vision that is the treasure of your heart and running with it until it becomes a reality.

My prayer is that the wisdom and knowledge you receive from this book will enable you to shatter the glass ceiling that has been hindering you from living supernaturally. I trust that you will discover your calling in life and begin to live your life on purpose. Today is the day to begin living in God's image as you were created to be, moving from ordinary to extraordinary, from one level of faith to another, from glory to glory, as this Scripture says:

> But we all, with open face beholding as in a glass the glory of the Lord, are changed into the same image from glory to glory, even as by the Spirit of the Lord.
>
> 2 Corinthians 3:18 KJV

By doing this, your life will surely count for something and make a difference in the lives of those around you.

Chapter 1

Value the Power of Vision

{ }

"Vision is a mental picture of a future state."

Casey Treat

Did you know that many people today live in one of two realms, neither of which exist? These two realms are the past and the future. Why do they live this way? Primarily because they do not understand the need of a strategy for the present in order to leave the past and powerfully step into a better future.

Some people remain chained to a past that never allows them to experience the fresh beginnings of a new day. Others relish the future but choose to ignore the present in hopes that it will disappear. What they lack is vision—a strategy that provides the entryway to living the abundant life God has promised them. People of vision understand that the past is their teacher, the present is their opportunity, and the future is not their enemy or something to be shunned or feared.

Vision is the ability to see God's presence, perceive God's power, and focus on God's plan in spite of obstacles. Vision is not a complicated mystery that only a select few can unveil. Rather, the Holy Spirit gives vision to us. God wants every one of us to have the kind of vision that ignites our desire, gives us purpose, and motivates us toward accomplishment. Someone once asked Helen Keller, a woman born without sight or hearing, who impacted many lives as a leader and a stateswoman, "What can possibly be worse than being born blind?" She promptly responded, "Having sight without vision."[4]

The value of vision cannot be overstated. Don't allow this personally significant word to become something trite because of its overuse. Value the vision God desires to ignite in you, because His vision provides a strategy that guarantees a journey of fulfillment and joy. Step into what is already designed for you.

YOUR VISION IS YOUR FUTURE

Many years ago at a conference I heard Dr. David Yongi Cho, the pastor of one of the largest churches in the world, make a statement that challenged the course of my life then and that continues to be "a journey maker" for clarity in my life today. He said, "Show me your vision, and I'll show you your future." Then he said, "If you can't tell me about your vision, what you're saying is that you have no future; and if you can't describe your future, you're unclear about your vision."

This shocked me as I realized that by omitting one—a clear vision—I had automatically disqualified myself for achieving the other—a meaningful future. As a young college graduate, I had a great deal of knowledge, but I had no clear vision of my future. Only when I allowed God to paint a picture of my future on the tablets of my heart, did I begin to understand the power of vision. It was then that I saw my vision as a strategy to take me out of my present and into my future.

A BRIDGE TO THE FUTURE

Vision is an unformed bridge from the present to the future that leads you from where you are to where God knows you need to be. I like the way I once heard pastor and author Casey Treat define it. He said, "Vision is a mental picture of a future state." Vision is the force that invents the future, because it is the ability to see your dreams and desires before they manifest in the natural. If you can't see it in your heart and mind, you may just only be having a temporary thought, idea, or fantasy. Wishing that something might someday happen for your betterment is nice, but it is not enough. Having vision is seeing the invisible and making it visible with a tenacity and determination to never let it go, which many so easily do.

The key to having vision is "seeing" with spiritual eyes. When you *"see"* a vision, you "see" your desired future state, and it becomes the purpose of everything you do, motivating you every hour of every day. Undeniably, it is through the work of the Holy Spirit that this vision is made clear to you as He begins to breathe His understanding into you as this Scripture says:

> But there is a spirit in man, And the breath of the Almighty gives him understanding

Job 32:8

FOCUS = CLEAR VISION

Vision brings your future into focus. That word "focus" is the key to understanding what clear vision really is and why it is necessary to accurately see your future. Once you have a clear vision, you still need a strategy to bring it into reality. King Solomon once prayed, "...give Your servant an understanding mind and a hearing heart..." (1 Kings 3:9 AMP). This tells us there are two steps involved in a vision being formed and fulfilled.

Step #1: Having a hearing heart (the initial desire, dream, and vision).

Step #2: Having an understanding mind (strategy, direction, and pathway).

Let's examine how to apply these two steps in a practical way by defining a strategy that includes a mission, vision, and goals.

As a pastor, I want to see people transformed by the life-changing power of God into victorious Christians. That is the big picture and my mission in life, but unfortunately, I can't possibly reach everyone. When I focus my desire to a narrower scope, my vision is to build a local, New Testament church in Honolulu, Hawaii, that will make successful Christians out of as many people as possible by reaching them with the life-impacting message of Jesus Christ. Wanting to have a specific number of people attend our church every Sunday by a specified time period is a goal. Goals are simply "bite-size" pieces of your vision that can be measured and attained. Without goals, a vision never goes beyond a dream.

Here are some practical examples of the differences between a mission, a vision, and a goal. Let's say your mission is to build a successful business. Your vision might be to build a car dealership and sell cars; your goal then could be to sell "x" number of cars each month. Someone else may have a mission to be a farmer. His vision is to grow wheat and his goal is to grow "x" number of bushels of wheat a year. Now do you understand how important it is to bring focus to your vision so you can set attainable goals to make it happen? Remember, a goal is simply a vision with a plan.

PEOPLE PERISH WITHOUT A VISION

How many Christians don't have a vision for their future, even though they have heard this statement numerous times? Unfortunately, too many! It was King Solomon, a man of great wisdom, who valued the power of vision and said, "Where there is no vision, the people perish" (Prov. 29:18 KJV). This Scripture does not mean that if you don't have a supernatural, visionary experience, you're going to physically die. It means that without a dream, a purpose, or a vision in your life, you are going to miss out on God's best. You will live entrapped by the enemy called "average" in a mediocre, lukewarm, status quo, maintenance mode. Where there is no vision, people talk about vague, mysterious things, but they never get focused on anything they can accomplish. They walk in circles, like the Israelites did in the wilderness, because they have no vision of their future. Moses had the vision, purpose, and direction, but the Israelites didn't; and that is why they got into so much trouble whenever Moses wasn't right there with them. They were constantly murmuring and complaining and were easily deceived. As a result, they found themselves wandering aimlessly in the desert for 40 years. Many died there because of their disobedience. Without Moses' vision from God, all of them would have perished and never entered into the Promised Land. Then Joshua would have been out of a job.

Vision helps you envision the future as it releases you from your past and causes you to look beyond the present. Again, let me remind you of Dr. David Yongi Cho's powerful statement, "Show me your vision, and I'll show you your future."

VISION: A MAP AND A COMPASS

Vision is like a map and a compass, the vital tools needed in times of decision to steer you in the right direction and keep your eyes on the destination. Here's a great story to illustrate this.

Two people went walking on a journey through the forest. One had in mind only a pleasant walk. The other had a destination, a map, and a compass. As the day passed and the shadows lengthened, both began to think of finding the edge of the forest.

The first, lacking a compass or map, said, "Just ahead is a mighty tree. From there, perhaps, I can see the way out of the forest." Walking to the tree and seeing no clear direction, the traveler looked toward another stronger looking tree that was not far away. He was sure it must be near the edge of the forest. From there, he could surely find his way out. But that tree gave no clue, either, to the way to the edge of the forest. Seeing many more sturdy trunks in the gathering twilight, the traveler reasoned, "If I go from tree to tree, surely I must find my way out of the forest at last." So the traveler wandered and wandered until darkness descended.

The second traveler also noted the gathering twilight. From her bag, this traveler pulled a map and compass. Aligning the map with the compass and taking a bearing from a rocky outcropping she could see through the trees, she set herself to walking true north—the way that would take her out of the forest, past the encompassing trees and to her evening's destination. At length, she found herself on the edge of the forest and on the road to her destination.[5]

Which traveler would you rather follow into the forest, the traveler who only had his eyes on the trees before him, or the traveler who had her eyes on a destination and was prepared with a plan to reach it? This question seems like a "no brainer," but many people end up wandering in the forest without a compass or a map for the majority of their lives. The good news is that vision is a strategy for taking charge of your life as it becomes a map and a compass to your future destination.

Wayne Gretzky was once asked why he was the world's greatest hockey player. He replied, "While most hockey players go to where the hockey puck *is*, I always go to where *I see* the hockey puck *will be*."[6] By seeing tomorrow today and living by the controlling factor called vision, we can anticipate and avoid many future problems and pitfalls.

ENVISION THE FUTURE AND RELEASE THE PAST

Vision is the force that invents the future when you rely on God's help to:

Envision a vision that

Evolves into a detailed plan,

Equipping you to implement an

Empowering strategy for life!

The future will be what you envision it to be. Vision is the desire that shapes your future, the desire to make something happen, the desire to change the way things are.

Walt Kallestad, the senior pastor of Community Church of Joy in Glendale, Arizona, is a man of vision having built a large church over the course of 15 years. Read what he says about the value of vision.

> "Whatever the size of your church or job or family, after the vision is shaped, people will be shaped by that vision. Great leaders know this. They are, therefore, people who shape their vision creatively and confidently. People like Walt Disney, Henry Ford, Thomas Edison, Mother Teresa, Margaret Thatcher, Martin Luther King, Jr., and numerous others were themselves shaped by the way they envisioned the future. Such is the power of vision. This power is a gift from God. God is greatly complimented when we envision what He envisions for us."[7]

A GIFT FOR ALL

This God-given gift of vision is not just for some believers; it is for *all* believers. God has a plan for you to prosper. If He said it, then it is true. He has something significant He wants you to accomplish in your life! It says so right here in this Scripture:

> "For I know the plans I have for you," declares the Lord,
> "plans to prosper you and not to harm you, plans to give
> you hope and a future."
>
> Jeremiah 29:11 NIV

We must believe He has a plan and go after it through faith and with patience by getting into His Word and trusting His way of doing things, as it says in Proverbs 3:5-6 TLB, "trust the Lord completely; don't ever trust yourself. In everything you do, put God first, and He will direct you and crown your efforts with success." His Word will renew our minds and we, too, can say boldly and courageously, like the apostle Paul said,

> We have the mind of Christ (the Messiah) and do hold the
> thoughts (feelings and purposes) of His heart.
>
> 1 Corinthians 2:16 AMP

How do you appropriate vision? Just apply these Scriptures to your life:

> Delight yourself also in the Lord, and He shall give you the
> desires of your heart.
>
> Psalms 37:4

Blessed is the man who walks not in the counsel of the
ungodly, nor stands in the path of sinners, nor sits in the
seat of the scornful; But his delight is in the law of the Lord,
and in His law he mediates day and night. He shall be like a
tree planted by the rivers of water, that brings forth its fruit
in its season, whose leaf also shall not wither; and whatever
he does shall prosper.

Psalm 1:1-3

"It is written, 'Man shall not live by bread alone, but by
every word that proceeds from the mouth of God.'"

Matthew 4:4

As you delight yourself in the Lord through reading and
meditating on His Word, He deposits His desires into your heart.
Your vision comes from Him, and He will bring it to pass.
However, vision is like a ladder; you climb it step-by-step in a
strategic manner.

To practice envisioning your future, follow these steps:

1) Expand your horizons by stretching your imagination.

2) Nurture new ideas.

3) Vote for positive changes with a welcoming attitude.

4) Imagine the impossible.

5) Stay ahead of tomorrow.

6) Invent the future.

7) Operate expectantly.

8) Notice unlimited opportunity.

TAKE YOUR TEMPERATURE ON VISION

I want to stir you up right now by asking you a question that will gauge your temperature concerning vision. Are you striving just to simply survive, are you dreaming about success without direction, or are you clear about the significant difference you will make on your current path? If all you are doing is striving to survive or just dreaming without substance about success, you don't have a vision and really don't comprehend its importance. Let me share with you what Helen Keller once said:

> "I am only one, but I am one,
>
> I cannot do everything, but I can do something.
>
> What I can do I ought to do,
>
> What I ought to do, by the grace of God **I will do.**"[8]

Helen Keller knew the power of vision as well as the danger of having physical sight without vision. She knew that her vision was her future. She could have wallowed in darkness and self-pity, but she chose to be a light to everyone she touched. Helen Keller chose not to live in the lofty heights of empty clouds and made a significant difference in peoples' lives because her vision had a purposeful direction and end result.

WHAT YOU SEE IS WHAT YOU GET

John C. Maxwell said this about vision in his book *Developing the Leader Within You:*

"*What you see is what you can be.* This deals with your potential. I have often asked myself: Does the vision make the leader? Or, does the leader make the vision?

"I believe the vision comes first. I have known many leaders who lost the vision and, therefore, lost their power to lead. People do what people see. That is the greatest motivational principle in the world. Stanford research says that 89 percent of what we learn is visual, 10 percent of what we learn is auditory, and 1 percent of what we learn is through other senses.

"In other words, people depend on visual stimulation for growth. Couple a vision with a leader willing to implement that dream and a movement begins. People do not follow a dream in itself. They follow the leader who has that dream and the ability to communicate it effectively. Therefore, vision in the beginning will make a leader, but for that vision to grow and demand a following, the leader must take responsibility for it."[9]

God told Abram (later renamed Abraham) when He showed him the land of Canaan, "What you see is what you get!" He didn't use those exact words, but the meaning was the same as we read here:

And the Lord said to Abram, after Lot had separated from him: "Lift your eyes now and look from the place where you are—northward, southward, eastward, and westward; *for all the land which you see I give to you and your descendants forever.*

And I will make your descendants as the dust of the earth;
so that if a man could number the dust of the earth, then
your descendants also could be numbered. Arise, walk in the
land through its length and its width, for I give it to you."

Genesis 13:14-17

God gave Abram the vision of the Promised Land, but he had to take possession of it as he obediently walked it out. Abram believed for it by faith not only for himself, but also for his descendants, none of whom existed at that time. Each person must personally take possession of God's vision and believe in faith for it to come to fruition.

IMPARTING VISION

People fit into one of four vision levels:

1) Wanderers: Those who never see it.

2) Followers: Those who see it but never pursue it on their own.

3) Achievers: Those who see it and pursue it.

4) Leaders: Those who see it and pursue it and help others see it.[10]

If you see the vision, it not only becomes your vision, but the vision or answer for people around you that God wills for you to reach. Abraham, Moses, Joshua, David, and every other great leader in the Scriptures caught God's vision and imparted it to their people. It is still happening in our times.

Luis Palau illustrated this point in his book *Dream Great Dreams:*

"Think about how nice and refreshing it is to taste a cold Coke. Hundreds of millions of people around the world have enjoyed this experience, thanks to the vision of Robert Woodruff. When World War II broke out during his tenure as president of Coca-Cola (1923-1955), Woodruff boldly declared, 'We will see that every man in uniform gets a bottle of Coca-Cola for five cents wherever he is and whatever it costs.'

"When World War II ended, Woodruff stated that before he died he wanted every person in the world to have tasted Coca-Cola. Robert Woodruff was a man of vision! With careful planning and a lot of persistence, Woodruff and his colleagues reached their generation around the globe for Coca-Cola. Robert Woodruff knew that what you see is what you get!"[11]

His vision is still being followed, as Coca-Cola became one of the first U.S. companies to enter the global market in China when the doors were opened for trade in the 1970s and in the former communist-bloc countries in Eastern Europe when the iron curtain fell in 1989.

Every great leader, who has achieved and accomplished admirable goals, which have had notable historic impact, was without exception a person of vision, not a person of chance. If you don't have a vision, you are, without a doubt, perishing!

DESIGN A NEW BLUEPRINT

No matter where you are, if you want to live at the next level in God's plan, you're going to have to design a new blueprint for your life by getting a fresh vision and seeing a new future. If you don't, you're going to keep getting what you've got. Even if you've never had a blueprint, a vision, for your life, it's never too late to write one if you simply understand these four things:

1) God has a future and a hope for you.

2) Without a vision, you will perish.

3) Your vision is your future.

4) It is up to you to change any negative vision.

Today is the day to stop thinking you are a victim. If your tree is producing crabapples, then change it! Jesus said, "Either make the tree good and its fruit good, or else make the tree bad and its fruit bad; for a tree is known by its fruit" (Matt. 12:33).

He was saying that as the tree, you are in control of your fruit. You can produce the kind of fruit that you want to produce, either good or bad. Even if up until now your fruit has been bad, today you can make a decision to change it for the good. You are not a victim. You are not under the control of some mysterious force that is holding you back. You are not stuck where you are. You can break out and bring forth whatever kind of life you want. The only thing stopping you is a lack of vision and the desire to pursue it.

WORDS SHAPE YOUR VISION

A vision begins to be shaped by the words of your mouth and the faith in your heart. A good indication of how strong your vision is begins by listening to the words you speak to yourself and to others around you. Are your words encouraging and uplifting and filled with life? Or, are they filled with despair and hopelessness or anger and bitterness? Your words are the containers, or carriers, that help shape and bring forth your vision. Here's what Jesus said:

> Brood of vipers! How can you, being evil, speak good things? For out of the abundance of the heart the mouth speaks. For by your words you will be justified, and by your words you will be condemned.
>
> Matthew 12:34,37

It's up to you to produce good fruit and to prepare your heart to have good treasure in it rather than evil by the words that you speak and the words that you allow to penetrate your ears.

> A good man out of the good treasure of his heart brings forth good things, and an evil man out of the evil treasure brings forth evil things.
>
> Matthew 12:35

What do you have in your heart? Fear? Worry? Statistics of your favorite baseball team? All the characters in "As My World Turns" or "Guiding Darkness"? None of that is going to produce good treasure. If your heart is full of junk, turn off the soap operas, MTV, and the radio, and turn on to God! Put down the newspaper sports section and pick up God's Word. Start listening to the words coming out of your mouth and change your conversation to words that produce life. Stop worrying and start leaning on God and seeking Him for the answers to your problems. Feed on faith, hope, and truth from the Word of God; deposit good treasure into your heart, and He will shape your vision.

YOU HAVE A HELPER

As the following Scripture says, the Holy Spirit will give you a vision of your future, tell you how to do it, and supply the ability and wisdom to bring it to pass—but it is up to you to pursue it:

> He, the Spirit of Truth...will guide you into all the Truth...He will tell whatever He hears [from the Father; He will give the message that has been given to Him], and He will announce and declare to you the things that are to come [that will happen in the future].
>
> John 16:13 AMP

VISION SPARKS ACTION

Your vision is the purpose, motivation, and drive behind all that you do. Examine your life. What gets you up in the morning? Is it vision or the alarm clock? Some people are at work at 8:00 A.M. because that's what time they are required to check in. Others are at work at 8:00 A.M. because they want to write a book, build a church, produce a TV program, teach a child how to read, invent a new machine that will save lives, or paint a masterpiece. Here's a good illustration of this difference.

"Several years ago on an extremely hot day, a crew of men were working on the road bed of the railroad when they were interrupted by a slow moving train. The train ground to a stop and a window in the last car—which incidentally was custom made and air-conditioned—was raised. A booming, friendly voice called out, 'Dave, is that you?' Dave Anderson, the crew chief, called back, 'Sure is, Jim. It's really good to see you.' With that pleasant exchange, Dave Anderson was invited to join Jim Murphy, the president of the railroad, for a visit. For over an hour the men exchanged pleasantries and then shook hands warmly as the train pulled out.

"Dave Anderson's crew immediately surrounded him and expressed astonishment that he knew Jim Murphy, the president of the railroad, as a personal friend. Dave then explained that over 23 years earlier he and Jim Murphy had started work at the railroad on the same day. One of the men, half jokingly and half seriously, asked Dave why he was still working out in the hot sun and Jim Murphy had gotten to be president. Rather wistfully, Dave explained, 'Twenty-three years ago I went to work for $1.75 an hour, and Jim Murphy went to work for the railroad.'"[12]

Jim Murphy caught the vision of the railroad company and rode that vision to the top. Dave Anderson woke up each morning to the ringing of the alarm clock and came to work to earn an hourly wage and nothing more. Jim Murphy was a leader who had purpose and ambition. Dave Anderson was a wanderer with no direction or a follower at best.

This illustration is not to say everyone must become the president of the company, but it does point out that too many people are operating in maintenance mode and don't even realize it until years have passed by. The only purpose they see in life is to go to work when the alarm clock rings, hoping they will eventually get a raise so they can buy a car or a bigger house. That is the driving force behind much of what they do. They are so limited in their thinking that they can't relate to anything other than this maintenance mode, which has become their daily existence. For them, "maintenance" has become their vision—their glass ceiling. They are not living their life on purpose. Instead, the circumstances and situations they encounter drive their lives.

Vision is that purpose for life that is strong enough, real enough, and vivid enough to stir you to action. It will put you through four or more years of college. It will take you through long workdays without being weary. It will keep you from despising the days of small beginnings.

Without vision, there will be no spark—just a status quo, maintenance lifestyle. You will end up doing what you think you *should* do instead of what you were *created* to do. Doing what you *should* do gets old quickly. Doing what you were *created* to do is exciting. Vision is the motivation; it's the desire to do what God created you to do.

VISION IS THE POWER OF YOUR LIFE

Without vision or revelation of what God wants a person to do in life, one tends to feel powerless. Such a person begins to wander aimlessly without direction and is never sparked to action. God loves us, and He knew that we needed revelation to keep us focused and directed toward His purposes, because without it, we would wander like lost sheep as these Scriptures tell us:

> Where there is no revelation, the people cast off restraint;
> but happy is he who keeps the law.
>
> Proverbs 29:18

> But when He saw the multitudes, He was moved with
> compassion for them, because they were weary and
> scattered, like sheep having no shepherd.
>
> Matthew 9:36

To be *weary* is to be sickly, weak, harassed, confused, frustrated, and beaten down—*perishing*. To be scattered is to be wandering through life with no purpose, no direction to keep us on course, no restraint—just drifting or floating along aimlessly and haphazardly, getting nowhere fast. To have no vision is like being in a boat out in the middle of a lake when the motor has quit and a storm is brewing. There is no power to keep the boat moving or to allow you to steer into the waves. Before long, the waves begin to control the boat, eventually capsizing it. Without a vision in life, you have no power to face the storms that come along or move in the direction you want to go. You have nothing to keep you focused, and you end up drifting until you are capsized and have missed out on much that God has for you. With a vision, you have the power to stay focused on a purpose that brings you through storms and keeps you from capsizing. It steers you toward success.

I am convinced that the reason some people fail in marriage is because they never had a vision for a successful, happy marriage. They only had a vision to marry. It's easy to get married. It's another story altogether to have a long-term, happy, successful marriage. Both partners must have the same vision so that when the storms come, they don't get weary and wander apart. If they don't embrace or possess the same vision, there is nothing to keep them focused and on course together. As a pastor, I've heard this statement too often from troubled spouses, "We just don't have anything in common anymore." That is sure proof they had no vision for the marriage.

WEATHERING THE STORMS

Vision gives you hope, purpose, and direction to power you through the storms of life. During the Vietnam War, many American military men spent years in prisoner of war camps living in horrible, tortuous conditions. The ones that had a vision, a purpose, and a hope of something ahead at their homecoming were able to handle the pressure and stress of all that came against them. They came home and moved on with their lives. But the ones who lost their purpose and hope and didn't have something or someone waiting at home either died in the camp or faced serious mental problems once they were released.

Major F. J. Harold Kushner was a prisoner of war in North Vietnam for five years. In describing his experiences as a POW, he shared the story of a young Marine who believed the camp commander when the commander told him if he would cooperate with the Viet Cong, he would be released. For two years, this marine was a model prisoner and led the camp's thought-reform group. After a couple of years, the Marine realized the commander had lied and wasn't going to let him go. As this reality got its hook into the young soldier, he became like a zombie, refusing to work or to eat. All he would do was lay on his cot sucking his thumb. He died after a few short weeks.[13] He had lost all hope. Hopelessness can kill.

CATCH THE VISION

When we value the power of vision, vision begins to replace what we see as obstacles. Vision replaces mental resistance, or strongholds that are built up in our minds. We've all become too familiar with echoes that say, "I've tried that before and it doesn't work." Or, "I've always done it this way." Or, "I'm too old to change now." We must challenge such limiting mind-sets that inhibit the potential greatness that lies within all of us. God knows where we are, He knows where we need to be, and He knows how to get us there. We simply must catch His vision, rise up, and walk it out.

FAITH AND HOPE—POWER PARTNERS

Now faith is the substance of things hoped for, the evidence of things not seen.

Hebrews 11:1

Faith and hope are two power partners that keep vision alive. Faith says, "I can live out of my imagination, instead of my memory." Faith says, "I can tie myself to limitless potential instead of my limiting past." Faith is the weapon that shatters the glass ceiling of hopelessness and limitations. It looks above and beyond ordinary circumstances and believes for extraordinary results. Faith holds on to hope for the future no matter how bad the present may be. Faith enables you to discover your purpose. It sees God's plan come to pass.

Hope is a picture of where we are going. It is a mental attitude and expectancy of the future. Hope says, "Never give up!" It is the anchor that keeps us focused in our mind, will, and emotions until what is invisible becomes visible as this Scripture says:

> This hope we have as an anchor of the soul, both sure and steadfast....
>
> Hebrews 6:19

Abraham Lincoln's early years didn't point to the White House. He faced many disappointments and failures, which didn't seem to make him a likely candidate for the presidency. Lincoln didn't allow his hope to die even though he couldn't see anything positive in his present circumstances. He told this story of how his dream to be a lawyer unfolded in a most unusual manner as he caught God's vision for his future calling.

"On the front porch of his little country store in Illinois stood Abraham Lincoln with Berry, his partner, who asked, 'How much longer do you think we can keep going?'

"Lincoln answered, 'It looks like our business has about winked out.' Then he continued, 'You know I wouldn't mind so much if I could just do what I want to do. I want to study law. I wouldn't mind so much if we could sell everything we've got and pay all our bills and have just enough left over to buy one book, *Blackstone's Commentary on English Law,* but it doesn't look possible.'

"Just then, a strange looking wagon came up the road. The driver drove it up close to the store porch, and the man looked up at Abraham Lincoln and said, 'I'm trying to move my family West and I'm out of money. I've got a good barrel on here that I could sell for fifty cents.' Abraham Lincoln's eyes went along over the wagon and came to the wife looking up at him pleadingly with her face thin and emaciated. Abraham Lincoln ran his hand into his pocket and took out, according to him, 'the last fifty cents I had,' and said, 'I reckon I could use a good barrel.'

"All day long the barrel sat on the porch of that store. Berry kept chiding him about it. Late in the evening, Abraham Lincoln walked out and looked down into the barrel and saw some things in the bottom of it—papers he hadn't noticed. His long arm went into it, fumbled around, and hit something solid. He pulled out a book and stood petrified. It was the *Commentary on English Law* by Blackstone.

"Now these are Abraham Lincoln's words: 'I stood there holding the book, looking up toward the heavens. There came a deep impression on me that God had something for me to do. He was showing me now that I had to get ready for it. Why this miracle otherwise?'"[14]

What would you do if you could sell everything you had and start a new life? Your answer to this question will reveal significant clues to your perceived vision and purpose.

WHOSE PLAN ARE YOU FOLLOWING?

Everyone has a vision, good or bad, positive or negative, godly or ungodly. There are two kinds of vision:

1) Vision from the world is self-oriented and focuses on "what I can *get*."

2) Vision from God is people-oriented and focuses on "what I can *give*."

Here is a good way to test the waters to determine if your vision is based on God's plan as outlined in His Word or if your vision is from the world. If your vision is from the world, it usually has to do with fleshly satisfaction and gratification—fame, fortune, position and power, and material possessions. If it is from God and His Word, it speaks of love, joy, peace, prosperity in every realm of life—spirit, soul, and body—and a desire to help others. The Word of God will give you a vision of success spiritually, mentally, physically, financially, domestically, and socially. It is a realization of God's purpose, plans, dreams, and desires for your life.

SEVEN STEPS TO ACTIVATE THE POWER OF VISION

Here are seven important steps to follow to activate your vision:

Step One: Invest time in prayer and hearing from God.

Establish a daily time of prayer in your schedule and make it a priority. If you truly want to know God's will for your life, you must spend time with Him in prayer seeking His wisdom and revelation. Ask the Holy Spirit to enlighten the eyes of your understanding as He speaks to you and helps you find the hope of your calling in Christ. Then stop talking and *listen* for His answers.

The most powerful form of prayer is to pray the Word and insert your name or the name of others into the Scripture. Here is an example of the prayer Paul prayed for the Ephesian Christians modified as a personal prayer.

I pray "that the God of our Lord Jesus Christ, the Father of glory, may give to *me* the spirit of wisdom and revelation in the knowledge of Him, the eyes of *my* understanding being enlightened; that *I* may know what is the hope of His calling, what are the riches of the glory of His inheritance" (Eph. 1:17,18).

In the fast-paced world in which we live, our time with the Lord often gets pushed aside. Don't despise small beginnings. Start with what you can do, even if it is just 5 or 10 minutes. Find a place where you can be alone and not be interrupted. You may need to set the alarm a little earlier before everyone else gets up, take your coffee break and go for a walk, or give up time in front of the TV after dinner. Do what works for you and don't let condemnation tear you down if you miss a day. Interruptions do happen.

Once you establish a pattern, you will find ways to stick with it. Be creative. God hears you wherever you are, and He will speak to you in unexpected places—in the car, the shower, the laundry room, your office. You may be surprised how easy it is to incorporate your prayer time into each day if you give yourself the freedom to look for new opportunities. This is about developing an intimacy with your loving, heavenly Father, not about religious protocol.

Step Two: Meditate daily on God's Word and His will for your life.

Implant the Word of God into your heart and mind every day. The more you meditate on (ponder in your heart and dwell on) God's Word, the clearer His will for your life will be. His promises are yours *if* you do what His Word says to do. Choose one verse a day to memorize and meditate on. If you don't put the Word into your heart, you won't have anything to draw upon when you need it. Here is what the Scripture says will happen:

> This Book of the Law shall not depart from your mouth, but you shall meditate in it day and night, that you may observe to do according to all that is written in it. For then you will make your way prosperous, and then you will have good success.
>
> Joshua 1:8

> Now this is the confidence that we have in Him, that if we ask anything according to His will, He hears us. And if we

know that He hears us, whatever we ask, we know that we have the petitions that we have asked of Him.

1 John 5:14,15

Step Three: Discuss your vision with people of faith.

God's Word clearly tells us to do this:

Where there is no counsel, the people fall; but in the multitude of counselors there is safety.

Proverbs 11:14

Pray and ask the Lord with whom you should share your vision. Seek those people of "like" faith that can pray in covenant agreement with you and discuss your vision in a nurturing, positive way. If you are married, it is important to discuss your vision with your spouse and come into agreement in prayer.

Insulate yourself from negative people and negative ideas. Stay clear of negative-thinking "experts." Remember, in the eyes of average people, average is always considered outstanding. Just because someone is a believer doesn't mean that person is of "like" faith. Beware of people who say things like, "I know someone who tried that and failed." Or, "You can't do that. It's never been done before."

As you seek godly counsel and wisdom, be sure you keep your heart open to correction and direction. Sometimes we can't see the forest for the trees, and we need someone who is wise and impartial to point out danger or pitfalls we don't see. This isn't the same as being negative. Pray about the counsel you receive, and let the Holy Spirit confirm it in your heart.

When you surround yourself and affiliate with people of faith and prayer, you enter into the God-ordained power of agreement as this Scripture says:

> Two can accomplish more than twice as much as one, for the results can be much better. If one falls, the other pulls him up; but if a man falls when he is alone, he is in trouble. And one standing alone can be attacked and defeated, but two can stand back-to-back and conquer; three is even better, for a triple-braided cord is not easily broken.
>
> Ecclesiastes 4:9,10,12 TLB

Step Four: Write down your vision simply and concisely.

It is important to put it in writing.

> And the Lord said to me, "Write my answer on a billboard, large and clear, so that anyone can read it at a glance and rush to tell others."
>
> Habakkuk 2:2 TLB

Remember what you read earlier about the difference between a mission, a vision, and a goal. Once you write down your vision, then you must break it down into bite-size goals, or the steps needed to bring it to pass. A vision without a plan will never move you into your future. As you write out your goals, be sure to establish checkpoints along the way to measure your progress.

If you are not skilled at setting or writing goals, there are many excellent goal-setting systems available. Do some research and find one that works well for you. Becoming a successful goal setter will change your life.

Step Five: Believe in the vision God imparts to you.

God's Word clearly gives us direction on this:

For assuredly, I say to you, whoever says to this mountain,
"Be removed and be cast into the sea," and does not doubt
in his heart, but believes that those things he says will be
done, he will have whatever he says.

Mark 11:23

You must align your actions and confessions with your faith. Faith without corresponding action is dead. You won't be motivated to action unless you first believe in what you are trying to do.

Step Six: Own the vision.

Your vision is unique to you. Don't try to copy someone else's vision. You must embrace ownership of your vision and speak life over it daily. Consider these Scriptures:

God...calls those things which do not exist as though they did.

Romans 4:17

Death and life are in the power of the tongue: and those
who love it will eat its fruit.

Proverbs 18:21

If you don't take ownership of your vision, no one else will embrace it either.

Step Seven: Exercise and endure until the vision comes to pass.

God has perfect timing, and we must align ourselves with His timing as it says here:

But these things I plan won't happen right away. Slowly,
steadily, surely, the time approaches when the vision will be
fulfilled. If it seems slow, do not despair, for these things
will surely come to pass. Just be patient! They will not be
overdue a single day!

Habakkuk 2:3 TLB

Therefore do not cast away your confidence, which has
great reward.

For you have need of endurance, so that after you have done
the will of God, you may receive the promise.

Hebrews 10:35,36

God has a time and a season for all He has promised to
come to pass. God's calendar is based on eternity while ours is
based on the here and now. Our expectations of time never seem
to match up with His. Be patient and wait on Him because His
timing is always perfect. The promises of God are "Yes and
Amen!" And they are conditional upon our obedience.

PLANT THE VISION

In order to produce results, we must first plant the vision in
our hearts just as a seed must be planted in the ground to produce
a harvest. Then we have to discipline ourselves and remain committed to nurture the vision by praying and meditating on the
Word of God, the same way a farmer waters and fertilizes his
plants. We have to fight against distractions and lack of faith like a
farmer fights to keep the weeds out of his ground. Lastly, we must
guard our hearts to keep them soft and pliable so the vision can

grow and multiply. If we remain faithful to God's plan, the harvest will come as this Scripture says:

> Still other seed fell on good soil. It came up, grew and
> produced a crop, multiplying thirty, sixty, or even a
> hundred times.
>
> Mark 4:8 NIV

God's "seed" principle of sowing and reaping governs every aspect of life. Nothing is an overnight success in the kingdom of God or in the natural realm on earth. Everything begins with a seed that will only grow if it is planted in fertile soil and properly nurtured. Every seed has a growing season before it matures and is ready for harvest.

God created everything with potential, including you. In essence, what you see today is not all there is. You have potential waiting to be tapped. God has given you vision to see beyond your present reality by giving you a picture in your mind's eye of the way things will be in the days to come. Your future is not just something that happens to you. Daring to challenge and rise above the pre-charted course of ordinary takes you to your future destiny. You, a child of God, were created to live above and beyond the ordinary. Reach out and capture your vision. Dare to live an extraordinary life driven to shape the future for God's glory.

TAKING ACTION TODAY

1) What are you doing to make a difference in the lives of those around you?

2) How do you plan to change the vision level (wanderer, follower, achiever, leader) at which you operate the majority of the time?

3) If "what you see is what you get," what are you planning to do to change what you are getting?

4) If you went on a treasure hunt inside your heart, what treasures would you find?

5) If you had the time, money, health, knowledge, and skill required to do anything you wanted, what would you do first?

6) What changes will you make in your daily routine to incorporate the seven steps for activating the power of vision in your life?

Chapter 2

Develop the Ways of a Winner

"Ability is what you're capable of doing.
Motivation determines what you do.
Attitude determines how well you do it."[15]

Lou Holtz

Unless you try to do something beyond what you've already mastered, you will never grow or live beyond where you are right now. Continual growth is the difference between winning and losing. A winner presses on to grow, change, and expand, always stretching beyond the ordinary. A winner knows his calling and purposefully strives to fulfill it. A person of mediocrity stops where it is comfortable and familiar, hiding beneath a glass ceiling of limitations and past defeats. Everyone knows you can't win a race if you stop and stand still.

A well-known country music star once expressed the importance of growth so well when she said, "You've got to continue to grow, or you're just like last night's cornbread—stale and dry." We ate a lot of cornbread at our house when I was a kid, and believe me, there's nothing drier than day-old cornbread. That's the way our lives are when we settle for an ordinary, status quo, mediocre life.

Do you believe you are the way you are because that's the way you want to be? Most people would deny this is true, but, in reality, they don't want to change badly enough to go beyond where they are and rise above the problems or circumstances of their lives. They cry and moan about where they are but don't want to do what it takes to get out of the "pity-party mentality" that keeps them there. They push the blame off on their environment, on events that have occurred in the past, or on people who have wronged them. They don't realize that if they keep on doing what they've always done, they'll keep getting what they've always gotten.

The reason most people don't change the way they are or what they are doing is because they lack motivation. I once heard someone say self-motivation is the power that raises a man to any level he seeks. We need to be motivated to grow, to take the next step up the ladder, or to climb the next hill. A winner learns three keys to staying motivated.

KEY #1: EVALUATE WHERE YOU ARE RIGHT NOW.

If you don't know where you are, you'll never know when you get to the next level. This is the time to search your soul and to ask the Holy Spirit to reveal to you where you are excelling and where you need to grow. Take a good look at your life and don't play the game of denial. Be honest with yourself as you answer these questions:

1)   What are you doing to grow spiritually?

2)   What are you doing to improve your relationships at home, at work, in your neighborhood, at church?

3) Are you satisfied with your physical health and fitness?

4) How balanced and in order are your priorities—God first, family second, and work third?

5) What is holding you back from growing in any area of your life?

6) Who or what is influencing or limiting you?

7) Is it small thinking, small planning, or small vision?

8) What power—past, present, or future—controls you?

9) What do you see as the treasure of your heart?

Write down the answers to these and any other questions that come to your mind. Knowing where you are is a springboard to taking you to where you want or need to be. It will motivate you to draw a line in the sand as a starting point for moving forward.

KEY #2: OVERCOME COMPLACENCY.

Complacency traps many people where they are. It has reached epidemic proportions in our society and, sadly enough, even in the church. We are so caught up with our daily routine that it takes a crisis to break us out of our comfort zone. Many of us know we need to lose weight and get in better physical condition, and at least once a month we promise ourselves we are going to change our eating habits and start exercising. Maybe we even go so far as to buy a treadmill or join a fitness center. All of our good intentions last a day or two, but before we know it, the treadmill sits idle or we just don't have time to go to the fitness center. Unfortunately, it often takes something devastating, such as a heart attack, before we seriously change our routine and habits.

Basketball coach Pat Riley once said, "Complacency is the last hurdle any winner, any team must overcome before attaining potential greatness."[16] To develop the ways of a winner and be all that you can be, you must overcome complacency. A great marriage can fail because of complacency. If you want to accomplish God's plan in your life, don't slip into complacency.

The way to overcome complacency is to get off the plateau you are on and leave something behind. Someone once said, "One half of knowing what you want is knowing what you must give up before you get it."

My wife, Kuna, and I bought an exercise machine. I know that if I want to look like the picture says I can look, I have to give up a certain amount of time each day to get on that machine *and* let go of my soda pop. I am the only one who can make the decision to defeat complacency and improve my health and fitness. What are you willing to give up to win over complacency?

KEY #3: DO WHAT YOU CAN DO TODAY TO COME CLOSER TO YOUR POTENTIAL TOMORROW.

Rome wasn't built in a day. You can't change everything about your life overnight. The best way to stay motivated and to win your race is to just keep doing a little extra each and every day. When you approach moving from where you are in bite-sized steps, before long you will find yourself where you want to be. Take that little extra effort and do what you can do today.

PERSISTENCE PAYS OFF

When I first looked at that exercise machine, it was real intimidating. My mind and my body weren't sure they were ready for it. I decided to approach it gradually—five minutes, then ten minutes, and before long, I could do 30 minutes; and it didn't seem so bad. If I missed a day, I just got back with it the following day. With persistence, it paid off. The difference between ordinary and extraordinary is that little extra "oomph," that little extra effort.

MEASURE YOUR PROGRESS

If you want to obtain different results, you have to take action and do something different than what you are doing now. Once you know where you are and where you want to be, set specific goals with established markers to measure your progress in getting to where you are going.

A runner always knows what race he is going to run. When Olympic gold medallist Michael Johnson steps up to the starting line, crouches in position, and waits for the gun to go off, he doesn't suddenly stop and ask the officials how far he has to run. He already knows if he is running a 100-meter or a 400-meter race and paces himself accordingly.

When I played soccer in high school, I started out playing defense. Then I decided I wanted to play a forward, offensive position. I talked to the coach, and he said, "Okay, if you really want to play this new position, you're going to have to become a better runner and build up your endurance." I had to act on what the coach said and do different things than I had been doing in order to prove to my coach I could perform on the offensive line. I worked on my running speed and endurance and ran through the cones to improve my agility. I learned new skills to be proficient in a new position. That is the way it is in life; if we want to see different results, we have to be willing to change what we are doing and learn new skills if necessary.

ATTITUDE DETERMINES PERFORMANCE

When it comes to winning or losing a race, the three things that determine which runner makes it across the finish line first are ability, motivation, and attitude. However, attitude is most often the deciding factor because an individual's attitude determines performance. The runner who has a "Yes, I can!" attitude is the one who presses on against all odds to win the prize. A winning attitude is a matter of choice.

Just as a pilot has an instruction manual for "flying attitudes," we have an instruction manual for "living attitudes"–the Bible! How does your attitude measure up to this Scripture?

> Do nothing out of selfish ambition or vain conceit, but in humility consider others better than yourselves. Each of you should look not only to your own interests, but also to the interests of others. Your attitude should be the same as that of Christ Jesus.
>
> Philippians 2:3-5 NIV

You may have thought you spotted a "typo" when you read about "attitude" flying manuals. Did you think it was supposed to be "altitude"? I was surprised as well when I read John Maxwell's story of how he discovered flying "attitude" determines a plane's performance. Here is his story:

"It was a beautiful day in San Diego, and my friend Paul wanted to take me for a ride in his airplane. Being new to Southern California, I decided to see our home territory from a different perspective.

"We sat in the cockpit as Paul completed his instrument checks. Everything was A-Okay, so Paul revved the engines, and we headed down the runway. As the plane lifted off, I noticed the nose was higher than the rest of the airplane. I also noticed that while the countryside was truly magnificent, Paul continually watched the instrument panel.

"Since I'm not a pilot, I decided to turn the pleasure ride into a learning experience. 'All those gadgets,' I began, 'what do they tell you? I notice you keep looking at that one instrument more than the others. What is it?'

"That's the attitude indicator," he replied.

"How can a plan have an attitude?"

"In flying, the attitude of the airplane is what we call the position of the aircraft in relation to the horizon."

"By now my curiosity had been aroused, so I asked him to explain more.

"When the airplane is climbing," he said, "it has a nose-high attitude because the nose of the plane is pointed above the horizon."

"So," I jumped in, "when the aircraft is diving, you would call that a nose-down attitude?"

"That's right," my instructor continued, "Pilots are concerned about the attitude of the airplane because that indicates its performance."

"Now I can understand why the attitude indicator is in such a prominent place on the panel," I replied.

Paul, sensing I was an eager student, continued, "Since the performance of the airplane depends on its attitude, it is necessary to change the attitude in order to change the performance."

He demonstrated this by bringing the aircraft into a nose-high attitude. Sure enough, the plane began to climb and its speed decreased. He changed the attitude and that changed the performance.

Paul concluded the lesson by saying, "Since the attitude of the airplane determines its performance, instructors now teach *attitude* flying."[17]

An attitude is defined as "an inward feeling expressed by an outward action or behavior." That is why attitudes can be "seen" without a word being spoken. We all recognize "the pout" of someone who is sulking or the "jutted" jaw of determination. Barbara Johnson, a humorous Christian writer, calls this "Sportin' a 'Tude!" Of all the things we wear, our expression is the most important because it clearly depicts our attitude.

Joseph, the twelfth son of Jacob written about in Genesis 37, is a biblical example of a believer who refused to live by the limitations of other people. He refused to compromise the treasure of his heart and even refused to accept his own limitations. The way he was able to do this was by keeping a righteous attitude no matter what circumstances came against him or what others said or did to him. It was his attitude that brought him favor in the eyes of God and man, which eventually brought him from the pit to the palace.

As a young boy, God gave Joseph a dream that built a treasure in his heart for the future that would take him far beyond the ordinary, status-quo life of his family. A dreamer is able to envision doing something bigger than life. Joseph made the mistake of telling his dream to his brothers who were "dream haters," those who are spiteful and envious of anyone trying to do big things. They hated Joseph so much that they threw him in a pit and later sold him to Egyptian slave traders. Be careful with whom you share your dream or vision. Dream haters will do everything they can to kill your dream.

Joseph held God's vision in his heart. Even in the most difficult circumstances, he never gave up on God. Because of his desire to follow after God and his determination to live in purity and holiness, which included keeping a righteous attitude, Joseph gained favor wherever he went. He was elevated to the highest position in Potiphar's household. When Potiphar's wife tried to seduce him, Joseph refused to yield to her temptation. For that, he was sent to prison for several years. In prison he made the best of his situation and was placed in authority over the other prisoners. Later when he was brought before Pharaoh to interpret a dream, Joseph was rewarded by being made second-in-command over all of Egypt. It was from this position that Joseph was able to save the lives of his family and see the fulfillment of the dream he had as a child.

No one said bringing forth a good treasure is easy! Joseph went from the pit to the palace, but it wasn't a pleasant journey getting there. No matter what came his way, Joseph kept his dream alive and kept serving God. He knew it wasn't the circumstances controlling his life; it was what was inside his heart that controlled his destiny. Joseph first had to have good treasure in his heart before it could come out of him. He kept his attitude right before the Lord, took whatever action was necessary in the face of every adversity, and never gave up until he saw the fulfillment of his destiny.

David had a "Christ-like" attitude. He didn't focus on the "should have," "would have," or "what if's" of life. Most importantly, he didn't blame others for what happened to him or for the circumstances in which he found himself. He forgave those who hurt him and was not vengeful. He kept his eye on the goal and focused on his relationship with God. David was a dreamer, a visionary, but he wasn't a daydreamer walking around with his head in the clouds. His strategy was to live according to God's Word, and he walked it out in his daily life. He learned from adversity and built positive relationships wherever he found himself. His reputation was preserved even in the face of lies spoken against him. He had patience to wait on God for each step.

He inquired of the Lord before he spoke or moved ahead. David's attitude indicated his performance.

God gives you the gift or ability to do what He has prepared you to do. He leaves it up to you to develop the motivation and the "Let's do it!" and "I'm not quitting" attitude to triumph over circumstances and obstacles that would try to hold you back from moving to your next level of growth. How does your attitude compare with David's when you face adversity? What steps will you take to adjust your attitude in the future?

YOUR BEST IS YET TO COME

To develop the ways of a winner and live above and beyond the ordinary, you have to be willing to become a dreamer, a visionary, to go beyond the "norm." This means you have to reach beyond where you are right now regardless of what you may have already accomplished, because where you are is not all there is, and who you are is not all God created you to be. His best is yet to come.

When world cycling champion Lance Armstrong was diagnosed with testicular cancer, it had already spread to his abdomen, lungs, and brain.[18] The prognosis *appeared* to leave no hope for his cycling career and questionable hope for his survival. But Lance had a vision for winning that wouldn't give up. He bravely endured the painful cancer treatments that drained him of his energy and stamina, but he kept his eye on the future.

After battling the ravages of the disease and treatments, Lance had a decision to make—whether to get back on his bike or to retire. He didn't accept the limitations the doctors spoke about his cycling future or even any limitations he may have felt in his weakened body. With the encouragement of his soon-to-be wife, Kristin, Lance swallowed his fear of the cancer and began training again with a vengeance.

Against all odds, only two years after his diagnosis, with the world cheering him on, Lance triumphantly won the most grueling cycling event in the world—the 1999 Tour de France. God's best for Lance Armstrong went beyond his victory over cancer and beyond his past racing titles. It even went beyond winning the Tour de France. Lance held on to the treasure of his heart, his vision to win against all odds, and his victory is touching the lives of other cancer victims and many other people who are living in what appear to be hopeless situations.

GOD'S SPIRIT IN YOU IS WHAT MATTERS

The way of a winner is to recognize it's not the circumstances around you; it's the Spirit of God in you that matters! This is where we are most often defeated. God gives us a vision, but when hard times come, we stop dreaming and allow circumstances to control us and eventually defeat us.

Have you ever been fed up? Everyone has been there at one time or another, but I want you to remember this nugget of wisdom Tim Storey shared with our church:

"Don't let your 'fed up'

Convince you not to 'get up'

And say it's time to 'give up.'"

Fight your "fed up" by developing the ways of a winner—living like Jesus lived:

Be a "doer" of the Word. God has a simple success plan, but He expects us to carry it out by studying His Word, meditating on it over and over, learning it by heart so it influences every decision, and finally by aligning our actions with His commands.

> Do not let this Book of the Law depart from your mouth; meditate on it day and night, so that you may be careful to do everything written in it. Then you will be prosperous and successful.
>
> Joshua 1:8 NIV

"Doers" have an attitude. They believe in their God-given potential, have a clear focused vision, act by faith in God's grace, and are persistent enough to accomplish it.

Train yourself to speak the Word. Jesus continually spoke the Word because He knew the power that was in it. God's Word has the power to cancel your past, to conquer your problems, to change your personality, and to complete your purpose.

Create a new vocabulary about yourself. Jesus didn't walk around saying, "I'm poor," "I'm weak," "I'm nervous," "I'm afraid." Jesus spoke what God said to speak. "For I have not spoken on My own authority; but the Father who sent Me gave Me a command, what I should say and what I should speak. And I know that His command is everlasting life. Therefore, whatever I speak, just as the Father has told me, so I 'speak'" (John 12:49,50). If you want to live an extraordinary life, you must speak God's Word about yourself and God's purpose for your life.

Start seeing yourself as God sees you. Jesus knew who He was in the Father. He said, "Do you not believe that I am in the Father and the Father in Me? The words that I speak to you I do not speak in My own authority; but the Father who dwells in Me does the works. Believe Me that I am in the Father and the Father in Me" (John 14:10,11).

Just as Jesus is in the Father, so are we in Him as He said, "A little while longer and the world will see Me no more, but you will see Me. Because I live, you will live also. At that day you will know that I am in My Father, and you in Me, and I in you" (John 14:19,20). It is time to start seeing yourself as God sees you—a person of worth and value, created in His image to have dominion over all the earth.

The apostle John further confirms this as he wrote, "Whoever confesses that Jesus is the Son of God, God abides in him, and he in God...and he who abides in love abides in God, and God in him. Love has been perfected among us in this...because as He is, so are we in this world" (1 John 4:15-17). Start speaking out of your mouth who you are in Christ *and* believing it.

DISCOVER THE "NEW" YOU

God has a new definition of who you are. The old definition is your past so stop measuring yourself by who you used to be with all the old mistakes and failures. His new definition is your future. You may be a diamond in the rough right now, but God sees a brilliant sparkle inside you just waiting to burst forth into the light. You have an important part to play in His kingdom that will bring great joy to you and to those around you. As you are developing the ways of a winner, remember it's not where you start but where you finish that determines success.

TAKING ACTION TODAY

1) What were the three most important things you learned about yourself from answering the questions earlier in the chapter that determined where you are right now?

2) What do you need to give up to get where you want to be?

3) What specific step will you take today to come closer to your potential tomorrow?

4) How does the way you see yourself differ from the way God sees you?

5) What do you need to do to see yourself as God sees you?

6) How has persistence paid off when a "give up" spirit came on you?

Chapter 3

{ Thinking Right About Yourself }

"It's not who you are that holds you back,
It's who you think you are not."[19]
John Maxwell and Jim Dornan

If you had to give a ten-minute speech about yourself in front of an audience, what are some of the words you would use to describe yourself? Would your talk be an inspiration to those who are listening? Would you be able to fill up the full ten minutes with positive, truthful words about yourself? Would it make you uncomfortable to have to talk about yourself to others? The answers to these questions should be a good indication of whether you think *right* about yourself. If you can't think of uplifting, positive words to describe yourself, then you aren't seeing yourself as God sees you or thinking the way God thinks.

Pastor and author Chuck Swindoll tells a story of his family playing the "what if" game while driving in the car. He asked his four young children, "What if you could be anybody on earth, who would you like to be?"

One daughter said she wanted to be the Bionic Woman. Other family members shared their "what ifs." When it was his youngest son's turn, little Chuck Jr. was silent. Pulling up to a stop sign, Chuck looked down at his son who was sitting beside him in the front seat and said, "Chuckie, who would you like to be?"

Chuckie's unusual and refreshing response was, "I'd like to be me."

Chuck just had to ask, "Why do you want to be you?"

Without hesitating, he said, "I like me."[20]

How many of us spend our entire lives wishing we were someone else instead of accepting who we are and celebrating our uniqueness? By not liking who we are and not thinking *right* about ourselves, in essence, we are sending God the message that we don't believe He knew what He was doing when He made us.

DUMP THE JUNK

Have you ever heard it said that God don't make no junk? It's true, but many Christians don't believe it. They go through life carrying pieces of junk on their backs inscribed with words such as *humiliation, failure, rejection, stupid, ugly, clumsy, unworthy, inadequate, unlovable.* Such words are not found in God's vocabulary, but they are favorites of our enemy, the father of lies, Satan. So why do we allow ourselves to be beaten down by such lies? The answer is simply *wrong* thinking!

Right thinking thinks spiritually—the way God thinks. It is founded on truth. This Scripture tells us how God's thoughts and ways differ from our own.

For My thoughts are not your thoughts, nor are your ways
My ways, says the Lord. For as the heavens are higher than
the earth, so are My ways higher than your ways, and My
thoughts than your thoughts.

Isaiah 55:8,9

Wrong thinking is carnal thinking—unspiritual and warped.
It is a form of wisdom, without God's input, based on a trust in
your own ways versus His ways with a total disregard for His
viewpoint, as this Scripture demonstrates.

For you have trusted in your wickedness; you have said, "No
one sees me"; your wisdom and your knowledge have
warped you; and you have said in your heart, "I am, and
there is no one else besides me".

Isaiah 47:10

THE ILLUSION OF KNOWLEDGE

Wrong thinking is an illusion of knowledge. The definition of
illusion is "something imagined but not necessarily true, real or
factual." One example is thinking that what you may know is
enough or all there is to know. Another example is thinking that
what you've traditionally heard is the only way it could ever be.
Daniel J. Boorstin spoke wisely about wrong thinking when he
said, "The greatest obstacle to fresh discovery is not ignorance—it
is the illusion of knowledge."[21]

Sometimes our thinking becomes warped by limitations
placed on us by other people, by their unbelief, their small ways of
thinking, and by their doubts, borders, limits, and fears.

Sometimes we put limitations on ourselves and then close our eyes and pretend they don't exist. Such limitations are really barriers between what you "see" you are able to accomplish and where you actually are. What you see may be factual, real, and true, but unreachable because of the invisible barrier either you or someone else has erected in front of you. It is like a lady window shopper who is looking at and longing for a beautiful dress in the display window. She can see it, but she can't touch it unless she smashes the window and reaches through it. The key to right thinking is not only to see through to what you can be, but to also reach through and lay hold of what you can be by smashing through your limitations.

A BOX OF DESTINY

B.P. Burkland was a successful businessman in Seattle, Washington. He once sold the property on which the Seattle Space Needle now stands. B.P. shattered his limitations in his life by thinking right about himself, seeing the vision God had for him, and reaching through overwhelming limitations in order to be what he believed he could be.

At the young age of six or seven years old, B.P. contracted polio, a dreadful disease for which there was no treatment at that time. Within a few months, his body had become massively deformed and crippled, shriveling up and becoming useless. His family believed in God and in the Bible, but like many Christians, they never expected their prayers to be answered. Their faith wasn't strong enough to overcome what they saw the polio had done to B.P.'s body.

B.P.'s parents didn't know what to do with him. They placed a wooden box on the floor, and his mother would drag him from room to room throughout the day as she went about her housework. Sometimes she placed a mirror on the floor in front of him so he could entertain himself while he sat in his box.

One day B.P. sat in front of his mirror and *really* saw himself—he had a vision. B.P. saw himself running. Jesus appeared to him and told him that he would be healed, and that he would be able to walk and run. The key was that B.P. *saw* himself walking and running around completely healed. He captured that vision in his heart.

From that day on, B.P. started rocking his box trying to shatter the physical limitations put on him by the disease, the emotional limitations put on him by the doctors and his family, and the limitations of a victimized individual. He was still crippled, he still couldn't walk, and his legs were useless; but he rocked his box back and forth until he would fall over. Then he would crawl out of his box on his hands and elbows and start scooting across the floor.

His mother would see him and say, "B.P. get back in your box." She would pick him up and put him back in that box, but B.P. wouldn't stay there. All day long, he would rock his box. Every once in a while, it would fall over; and he'd start crawling. B.P. had a vision of getting out of his box!

For months B.P. kept rocking his box until he'd fall over, and then he'd scoot. Pretty soon he could scoot faster than his mom could catch him. Before long, he started scooting over to a chair, pulling himself up trying to get his legs under him, and then fall.

Day after day, week after week, and month after month, B.P. rocked his box and scooted until as a teenager, he began to walk and then run. As a young man, he lived without limitations.

Nobody knew that the successful businessman, B.P. Burkland, had spent his early years battling polio or that he had spent his early years living in a box—defined by others as his "box of destiny." Faced with impossible circumstances and limitations, B.P. Burkland rocked his box because he had seen a vision and believed the words Jesus spoke to him. B.P. smashed the glass ceiling of his limitations by thinking *right* about himself, keeping the vision in his heart foremost in his mind and then reaching for it. When his mother said, "B.P., get in your box," his vision rose up inside him saying, "No, you're not going to keep me in a box." His mother didn't understand it, but B.P. knew he couldn't let that stop him.[22]

We need to rock our boxes even if it means falling out and scooting, even if others around us don't understand it. Thinking *right* about yourself is not always popular; it will be challenging—to you and to others—but without a doubt, it will be rewarding.

BE A "NO-LIMIT" PERSON

Right thinking about yourself pleases God and can only be accomplished in faith—thinking His thoughts and not your own. It is thinking higher than your circumstances or problem. It is being a "no limit" person—someone who does not let the limitations that most people accept get in the way. It is seeing what God sees. B.P. looked in the mirror, but he didn't see a crippled, deformed body. He saw what Jesus saw: a young man walking and running, completely healed.

It is impossible to perform consistently in a manner inconsistent with the way in which you see yourself. If you do not see yourself as someone who is strong in faith, you won't become a faith-filled person. If you do not see yourself overcoming life's greatest challenges, chances are you won't. If you do not see yourself winning the race, you'll never be a champion. If you do not see yourself making a difference, you'll never change another's life.

Say this to yourself:

No doubts,

No borders,

No limits, and

No fears...only faith in Jesus.

Then memorize this Scripture:

I have strength for all things in Christ Who empowers me [I am ready for anything and equal to anything through Him Who infuses inner strength into me; I am self-sufficient in Christ's sufficiency].

Philippians 4:13 AMP

YOU ARE WHAT YOU THINK YOU ARE

Your thinking determines the level of your success. Scientists estimate we use 10 percent of the most awesome computer known to mankind—our brain. Therefore, if your thinking is operating at only 10 percent capacity and God's is unlimited; and if God says in 1 Corinthians 2:16 that you "have the mind of Christ"; and if Proverbs 23:7 says, "For as he thinks in his heart, so is he," why not choose to do what the Bible says? One reason we don't is because we have warped thinking from being carnally minded. We must be spiritually minded in order to think right about ourselves and please God.

> For those who live according to the flesh set their minds on the things of the flesh, but those who live according to the Spirit, the things of the Spirit. For to be carnally minded is death, but to be spiritually minded is life and peace. Because the carnal mind is enmity against God; for it is not subject to the law of God nor indeed can be. So then, those who are in the flesh cannot please God.
>
> Romans 8:5-8

LET TRUTH SHAPE YOU AND MAKE YOU

Another reason for warped thinking is that we don't possess a revelation of the greater One in us. Gaining such a revelation starts with allowing the Truth to make you and shape you.

> If you abide in My word, you are My disciples indeed. And you shall know the truth, and the truth shall make you free.
>
> John 8:31,32

Right thinking is truth-founded. It's not founded on human emotion or on emotional persuasion or on church tradition. It is founded on the Word of God allowing the truth to shape you and make you strong in the Lord who dwells in you.

Finally, my brethren, be strong in the Lord and in the power
of His might.

Ephesians 6:10

It is founded on the Word that says you are the righteousness of God in Christ Jesus.

For He made Him who knew no sin to be sin for us, that we
might become the righteousness of God in Him.

2 Corinthians 5:21

Jesus took our sin and paid for it on the cross so we could
become "the righteousness of God in Him." When we accept Jesus
as Lord, we are instantly born again in our spirits. However, our
minds are not instantly renewed and that is why we have such a
hard time thinking *right* about ourselves. We must renew our
minds with the Word in order to think like God thinks and fulfill
His will in our lives.

And do not be conformed to this world, but be transformed
by the renewing of your mind, that you may prove what is
that good and acceptable and perfect will of God.

Romans 12:2

It is time to get rid of warped thinking by renewing your
mind—getting a revelation of the truth of the Word about thinking *right* about yourself. Verse 3 of Romans 2 shows where some
Christians have become warped in their thinking, and I want to
clarify this for you.

For I say, through the grace given to me, to everyone who is
among you, not to think of himself more highly that he

{ 59 }

ought to think, but to think soberly, as God has dealt to each one a measure of faith.

Romans 12:3

Paul is speaking to the Christians in Rome and telling them they should be thinking God's thoughts about themselves, not their own carnal thoughts. "Not thinking of yourself more highly than you ought" does *not* mean you are a nobody, unworthy, or no good. If the Word says you are "the righteousness of God in Christ," then thinking of yourself as righteous is not thinking of yourself higher than you ought. That's the way you ought to be thinking—spiritually, God's way, in line with His Word.

BE FILLED WITH THE WORD DAILY

The only way to renew our minds and think the way God thinks is to fill our minds with the Word. That doesn't mean just going to church and listening to the pastor preach; it means personally reading the Word on a daily basis. If you don't have a daily time with the Lord studying the Scriptures, the battle in your mind will overwhelm you. If you aren't a reader, then get the Bible on audiocassettes and listen to it on tape.

WISDOM IS THE LIFE OF KNOWLEDGE

Earlier in the chapter we read Isaiah 47:10 that says, "Your wisdom and your knowledge have warped you." It is important to understand there are two types of wisdom: a heavenly wisdom from God and a worldly, demonic wisdom from Satan. When the wisdom comes from above, God speaks to your spirit—your heart.

Then there is a wisdom that looks like the accepted kind of counsel by the world's standards, but it isn't from God.

> Who is wise and understanding among you? Let him show by good conduct that his works are done in the meekness of wisdom. But if you have bitter envy and self-seeking in your hearts, do not boast and lie against the truth. This wisdom does not descend from above, but is earthly, sensual, and demonic. For where envy and self-seeking exist, confusion and every evil thing are there. But the wisdom that is from above is first pure, then peaceable, gentle, willing to yield, full of mercy and good fruits, without partiality and without hypocrisy. Now the fruit of righteousness is sown in peace by those who make peace.
>
> James 3:13-18

I want you to see that knowledge alone is not enough to renew your mind. Wisdom must be applied to knowledge so that you will bear the right kind of fruit in your life. In order for knowledge to have wisdom applied, you need the breath of the Holy Spirit.

> But there is a spirit in man, and the breath of the Almighty gives him understanding.
>
> Job 32:8

There is a spirit in man, but true wisdom comes from above when God speaks to your spirit, your heart. Without the Holy Spirit you will not be able to differentiate between godly wisdom and worldly wisdom, and your thinking will be wrong. The way to tell the difference is to check out the characteristics in the above

Scripture. Are you experiencing peace, or are you experiencing confusion and strife?

BATTLE OF THE MIND

God knows the battle that goes on in our minds. The glass ceilings that hold us back from seeing ourselves as God sees us, or thinking as He thinks, are strongholds that have been erected in our minds. Most often we don't even recognize them because we are looking at outward appearances instead of at the spiritual aspects of what is limiting us. We must confront these limitations if we are going to live our lives on purpose.

B.P. Burkland's parents saw the deformities of their son's flesh and blood body. The strongholds the enemy built in their minds told them B.P. would never get out of his box. It was B.P. who saw the vision God had for him and knew the battle was spiritual. He fought to keep his thinking focused on God's promise, not on what *appeared to be* his limitations. The vision—the treasure—in His heart fueled his faith until what wasn't seen manifested in the flesh.

God wants us to get rid of the *cannot* thinking that holds us back from seeing ourselves as He sees us. The key is to renew our minds and change our thinking from *cannot* to *can do,* as this poem reminds us:

> "If you think you are beaten, you are;
> If you think you dare not, you don't
> If you like to win, but think you can't
> It is almost certain you won't!
> If you think you'll lose, you're lost,

For out in the world we find
Success begins with a fellow's will;
It's all in the state of mind.
If you think you're outclassed, you are.
You've got to think high to rise.
You've got to be sure of yourself before
You can ever win a prize.
Life's battles don't go
To the stronger or faster man,
But sooner or later the man who wins
Is the man who thinks he can!"

Author Unknown

God has given us the weapons to fight against wrong thinking. They are spiritual weapons because our enemy—Satan—operates not in the flesh but in the spirit realm.

> For though we walk in the flesh, we do not war according to the flesh. For the weapons of our warfare are not carnal but mighty in God for pulling down strongholds, casting down arguments and every high thing that exalts itself against the knowledge of God, bringing every thought into captivity to the obedience of Christ.
>
> 2 Corinthians 10:3-5

The truth of the Word of God is the weapon that defeats every lie and deception that the enemy tries to use against the knowledge of God. The Word has the power to renew our minds, to tear down the strongholds, to bring our thoughts into *right* thinking and win the battle, if we will do what it says in James 1:19-26:

Hear it. "Let every man be swift to hear" (v. 19).

Receive it—the implanted Word. "Receive with meekness the implanted word, which is able to save your souls" (v. 21).

Do it. "Be doers of the word" (v. 22).

Don't deceive yourself. "And not hearers only, deceiving yourselves" (v. 22).

Continue in it. "He who looks into the perfect law of liberty and continues in it" (v. 25).

Forget not. "And is not a forgetful hearer but a doer of the work, this one will be blessed in what he does" (v. 25).

Bridle your tongue. "If anyone among you thinks he is religious, and does not bridle his tongue but deceives his own heart, this one's religion is useless" (v. 26).

BE A BOX ROCKER

God has a plan and a destiny for you. He has new levels of growth for you to rise to as you renew your mind and think *right* thoughts about yourself. Be a box rocker and shake yourself out of wrong thinking. Keep your vision—the treasure in your heart—in the forefront of your mind at all times so you can see through to what you can be. Wash your mind with the Word of God so that in faith you can lay hold of your destiny. Then identify and change—smash through—the limiting beliefs that have been holding you back from your greatest accomplishments by thinking *right* about yourself.

ESTABLISH YOUR FOUNDATION

Thinking *right* about yourself is a life or death decision! That is a pretty blunt statement, but it is true. God has told us to choose life or choose death, blessing or cursing.

> I call heaven and earth as witnesses today against you, that I have set before you life and death, blessing and cursing; therefore choose life, that both you and your descendents may live; that you may *love* the Lord your God, that you may *obey* His voice, and that you may *cling* to Him, for He is your life and the length of your days; and that you may *dwell in the land* which the Lord swore to your fathers, to Abraham, Isaac, and Jacob, to give them.
>
> Deuteronomy 30:19,20

No one can make this decision for us. We choose life (blessings) by the principles by which we choose to live. It is up to us to establish the right foundation for life by making the right choices. It is a gift from God to be able to change and rise above the difficult circumstances in life. The worst part of hell is, you're stuck there! The good news is that while we are on this earth, we still have the right to change what we are and who we are by making choices that will produce life and not death. Thinking right about yourself or having positive self-worth is the foundation of life— seeing value in yourself. You must value yourself worthy of God's best or you will never receive it.

When you refuse to believe in your own value, you declare a death curse on the purpose for which you were born—to love God, to obey His voice, to cling to Him, and to dwell in the land He has given you. If you don't love yourself, you can't love others, including God. We can't serve God or man without love. If we refuse to love ourselves, we are being disobedient to the Lord.

When God repeats a commandment in the Scriptures nine times as He has with "love your neighbor as yourself," we can be sure it is important.[23] If he had just said to love our neighbor, we might have been off the hook; but He was specific that we are to love ourselves. We read it once in the Old Testament.

> Do not seek revenge or bear a grudge against one of your
> people, but love your neighbor as yourself. I am the LORD.
>
> Leviticus 19:18 NIV

Let's read what Jesus said in Matthew, which was repeated in Mark 12:30-31 and Luke 10:27.

> Jesus replied: "'Love the Lord your God with all your heart
> and with all your soul and with all your mind.' This is the
> first and greatest commandment. And the second is like it:
> 'Love your neighbor as yourself.' All the Law and the
> Prophets hang on these two commandments.
>
> Matthew 22:37-40 NIV

It is pretty hard to argue with those words. The apostle Paul wrote that such love is the fulfillment of the law because it sums up all the other commandments.

> The commandments, You shall not commit adultery, You
> shall not kill, You shall not steal, You shall not covet (have
> an evil desire), and any other commandment are summed
> up in the single command, You shall love your neighbor as
> [you do] yourself. Love does no wrong to one's neighbor [it

never hurts anybody]. Therefore, love meets all the
requirements and is the fulfilling of the Law.

Romans 13:9,10 AMP

God made you special. You are conformed to the image of
Christ. You are a conqueror, an overcomer, a victorious warrior,
adopted as a son or daughter of the Most High God, blessed with
every spiritual blessing in the heavenly places in Christ, accepted
in the Beloved, and redeemed by His blood. Choose to live out
this awesome spiritual heritage by applying the principles you
have learned in this chapter and in the coming chapters. Think
right about yourself.

TAKE ACTION TODAY

1) What ten words best describe who you think
you are? (Write them down and be honest with
yourself.)

2) What ten words best describe who God says you
are? (Use your Bible if necessary and make a list
of the words and the Scriptures you find.)

3) What did you discover about your thinking when
comparing these two sets of words?

4) What junk (negative words or thoughts) do you
need to dump?

5) What specific steps will you take within the
next seven days to change the way you think
about yourself?

Chapter 4

{ Mastering the Art of Communication }

"It takes two to speak the truth.
One to speak and the other to listen."[24]

Henry Thoreau

Communication has the power to start or end a war; to make or break a marriage; to close a million-dollar business deal or lose it to a competitor; to build or destroy a friendship; to create intimacy with God or build an impenetrable wall. People must master the art of communication if they want to live in this world with any measure of success. Communication is a two-way street. It takes two people: one to speak and the other to listen, with both parties taking turns speaking *and* listening.

The communication industry has exploded over the past ten years. With every imaginable kind of high-tech gadget at their fingertips with which to communicate around the globe, many people still don't know how to communicate effectively. Many think that if they have lips and a voice, they're communicating. A good communicator must be able to get a point across clearly and concisely as if painting a picture in the other person's mind. Just because you know what you are saying doesn't mean everyone else understands you.

The late Dr. Reinhold Niebuhr spent considerable time and paper in writing out his theological position carefully explaining his philosophy, his credo. When he completed this profound and voluminous masterpiece, he decided to send it for his evaluation to a minister friend who was a more practical thinker with a pastoral "heart." This clergyman waded through the reams of paper, trying desperately to grasp the meaning of it all. Finally, he wrote Dr. Niebuhr this candid reply. It read,

"My dear Dr. Niebuhr:

I understand every word you have written, but I do not understand one sentence."[25]

Dr. Niebuhr was a brilliant man who knew the importance of communicating clearly. Perhaps he needed to be more concise, but at least he was wise enough to realize someone else with a more objective, practical eye should evaluate his material. He wanted it to be understood by others. Otherwise, all his words would have been in vain. By receiving this simple, direct feedback from the other minister, Dr. Niebuhr discovered he had not painted a clear picture in the mind of his reader.

It is our own responsibility to determine whether others around us understand what we are saying. If not, we need to learn how to choose our words more wisely. Mark Twain once said, "The difference between the right word and the almost-right word is the difference between 'lightning' and 'lightning bug.'"[26]

THE TONGUE OF THE LEARNED

Learning how to speak and when to speak are critical keys to effective communication.

The Lord God has given Me the tongue of the learned, that
I should know how to speak a word in season to him who
is weary.

Isaiah 50:4

That Scripture is a prayer each of us should pray for ourselves. We need to have the tongue of the learned to know what words to speak for each situation or season. Everyone goes through different seasons in life. It is important to be sensitive to what season someone is in before you speak. If you come home from playing the best golf game of your life and your wife has been taking care of three children suffering with the chicken pox, you'd better realize she isn't in the same season as you are. If you don't choose your words carefully, you'll find yourself in big trouble. As you learn to read what season someone is in, you will be better prepared to minister to them in their area of need rather than your own.

How many times has someone spoken to you, who was right in terms of what was being said, but the *way* it was said just set you off course? It may have been the tone of voice used or the body language or perhaps your season was different from theirs. This is how many arguments are started, especially between spouses and between parents and children. It is also the way misunderstandings separate friends, neighbors, business associates, and church members.

IT'S MORE THAN WORDS SPOKEN

Communication is much more than just the words spoken. Years ago a woman traveled to Paris and found a beautiful piece of jewelry she wanted to buy. She wired her husband saying, "I found the necklace of my dreams. It only costs $5,000. Can I buy it?" Her husband wired back, "No, price too high!" But when the wire service operator sent the message, the comma was left out. It read, "No price too high!" Omitting that comma caused quite a stir when she returned home wearing that necklace.[27]

Jesus knew how to speak with the tongue of the learned. The Scripture in Isaiah 50 was actually speaking prophetically about Him. Jesus read each situation He encountered and said the right thing at the right time. Sometimes He recognized that the best way to communicate was to say nothing. That's one that has been tough for me to learn.

I had been praying about learning how to communicate with my daughter, Ashley, who was growing up much too quickly before my eyes. One day, I happened to find Ashley crying about a situation with her mother in which she misunderstood what her mother had said to her. Ashley cries those big ol' crocodile tears, the kind you can hear hitting the ground and absolutely melt a daddy's heart! Just as I put my arm around her, the Spirit of God said, *This is your opportunity.*

I didn't feel like it was my opportunity, but I said, "Let's go to the next room and talk." I sat her right across from me, and we just looked at each other. I said, "Ashley, talk to me."

"I don't want to, Dad. I'm embarrassed."

"Ashley, come on talk to me."

"I don't want to, Dad."

She was still crying, and I knew it would do no good if I got stern and said, "Talk to me!" Nor was it the time to say, "Well, if you don't want to talk, I'll see you later." That wasn't what she needed.

I looked her in the eyes and said, "Come on, honey. You're important to me. What you have to say is important too. Talk to me."

It took about an hour of quietly sitting there with her and then talking to her to work through that situation and help her understand. It really was a good opportunity to try to figure out how to communicate with my growing daughter. I knew I had to learn it before she reached the teenage years.

Babies begin learning communication skills from the moment they leave the womb. They can't speak intelligible words, but they quickly learn how to make their needs and desires known with loud wails and crying. They express happiness and contentment with sweet gurgles and cute little smiles and giggles. Communication habits are quickly formed.

Parents learn to differentiate between a cry that says, "I'm hungry" from one that says, "I'm hurting" or from one that says, "I don't want to sleep right now. I'm just going to exercise my lungs for a while." If we listened as carefully as new parents do to their newborn, when we communicate with older children, spouses, business associates, or friends, many of our communication problems would disappear.

THREE LEVELS OF COMMUNICATION

Life is all about dealing with other people—those above, around, and below us. The art of communication means learning how to connect with people at any of these levels. Those above being a boss or someone in authority over you; those around being peer-level individuals; and those below being people who are looking up to you for leadership and guidance. We have to learn to talk with people at all three levels in their season and in a way that is appropriate to their level. You wouldn't talk to your boss the same way you talk with your three-year-old son. The Bible says, "The heart of the wise teaches his mouth, and adds learning to his lips" (Prov. 16:23).

ESTABLISH A CONNECTION

To be an effective communicator at any level, put yourself in the other person's seat, consider how each one thinks and feels and where each one is coming from in that particular situation. Ask yourself, "Am I connecting? Am I getting through?" Sometimes it means back-pedaling a bit instead of charging ahead if someone isn't connecting. Without a good connection, a discussion can lead to a debate, which leads to an argument and eventually a break in trust. It takes less time to slow down and build a solid connection with someone in the beginning than it does to have to go back and repair a damaged relationship.

Watch the way you talk so that the communication of your faith may be effectual as this Scripture says:

[And I pray] that the participation in *and* sharing of your faith may produce *and* promote full recognition *and* appreciation *and* understanding *and* precise knowledge of every good [thing] that is ours in [our identification with] Christ Jesus [and unto His glory].

Philemon 1:6 AMP

I communicate the Gospel to a believer in a much different way than I communicate it to an unbeliever. I was invited to speak at a Rotary Club meeting about spirituality in the marketplace. I knew walking into that environment what it was going to be like. These bankers and business executives were professionals in their own fields, and very few of them were Christians.

I didn't try to mislead them. I simply established where I was coming from and shared my perspective. I said, "I know I cannot speak on all spirituality in the marketplace because all spirituality in the marketplace is not good. My beliefs are different than many of yours; but I can only share from my perspective so let me do that."

As I talked with them I shared a lot of Scripture, but I didn't call out verse references or read from the Bible directly because I wanted to communicate biblical truths in a way in which we could connect. I knew they had an image of how I was going to speak to them. I could just hear some of them saying, "Here comes the preacher boy, and he's going to da-da-da-da!"

I explained how we operate our ministry as a corporation with integral business principles. I established myself as a CEO, a principal, and president of the corporation, then explained that I am a pastor first and foremost. I told them how many staff I had and some of the real, day-to-day challenges we face. I could see they were beginning to connect with me because I was talking on their level in a way they could relate with what I was sharing.

Once I established the connection, I was able to say, "Now this is how spirituality in the marketplace would fit for you from the biblical perspective...." They received what I was saying because I didn't go in there and say, "You all need to be saved, or you're going to hell." They would have walked out on me. If you want to be effective, you have to learn how to communicate with any given audience. Communicating in a different way is not compromising your message. It's learning how to be wise in communicating with a generation that is already skeptical and cynical.

People want to hear good news. The problem is that a lot of us have gotten our opinions involved in the message. It's not good news to them when all they hear is, "You are going to hell." We have to communicate love, joy, and peace to this dying generation that so desperately needs hope. They must also see fruit in our lives, or they won't buy in to our message. Trust is not easily given; it must be earned.

FIVE LESSONS ABOUT COMMUNICATION

Here are five lessons about communication that will change your life.

1: Miscommunication has the potential to change relationships.

Have you ever heard the old saying, "That which can be misunderstood will be misunderstood?" If you value relationships, you will embrace the truth of that statement and guard against it. Miscommunication almost always produces negative results. I quickly learned this from my wife, Kuna.

The household in which I grew up did not teach me how to communicate in a positive, uplifting manner. If anyone could be classified as a "non-communicator," my father was just that. That old kid's taunt, "Sticks and stones can break my bones but words can never hurt me," is a lie. Words leave deep wounds in our emotions, and I was definitely wounded.

When I got married, I did not know how to communicate in the same warm, affectionate way Kuna was used to in her family. She let me know up front that I was not treating her the way she wanted to be treated. Three minutes of conversation often erupted into a major argument.

Mutual respect is key to effective communication. I loved Kuna with all my heart, but my style of communication did not reflect the mutual respect and value I felt in my heart for her. I had to learn to express myself in a way that Kuna would not misunderstand my motives. I started listening to the words I spoke and changing what was coming out of my mouth to be more encouraging and positive. Because I knew she loved me, I was able to take Kuna's counsel to heart and work on improving my communication skills. It was a gradual, step-by-step learning process, but it was vital to building our marriage into what it is today.

The three things that destroy most marriages are poor communication, issues relating to sex, and finances. I'm not going to explore all of these, but it is important for you to know that good communication is not an option in a happy marriage.

We must understand the power of our words. The universe and all that is in it was created by God's spoken words. Now that's power! Likewise, our relationships and personal world around us are created by the words we speak or by the words others around us have spoken which we have believed.[28] This truth is clearly explained in Scripture:

> From the fruit of his mouth a man's stomach is filled;
> with the harvest from his lips he is satisfied. The tongue
> has the power of life and death, and those who love it will
> eat its fruit.
>
> Proverbs 18:20,21 NIV

Are you speaking life or death by the words you speak over yourself and others around you? Consider your words carefully. If you have been speaking death, repent and ask the Holy Spirit to teach you how to communicate in love. Old patterns can be broken and replaced. I know, because I've done it in my own life. It doesn't happen overnight. It is a process, but if you will humble yourself and submit to the leading of the Holy Spirit, you can change your life and your relationships.

2: When you go through someone else to get your message across, there is potential for problems.

Have you ever played the game "Gossip"? Everyone sits in a circle, and one person whispers a message to the person on the right. That person whispers the message to the next person until the message has been passed around the circle. The last person speaks out the message. Inevitably, the message at the end doesn't even resemble the message spoken by the person who started the game.

If you want to make a point, the best communicator is *you*. If you are intimidated or are challenged when talking to someone, it is probably an indication that you aren't communicating clearly or skillfully.

There are times when it is necessary to give instructions to someone else to carry out or a message that must be passed along to several people. In some cases, the best way to assure you have been understood is to ask the person to repeat back to you what you have said or asked them to do. Be careful how you do this. Don't give the other person any indication that you don't trust them or are talking down to them.

This is a very effective with children. Once they have repeated back your instructions or message, they can't use that age-old excuse, "I didn't hear you say that," or "I didn't understand what you wanted me to do." It holds the listener accountable.

A good communicator should be able to use this technique to avoid miscommunication in any conversation. One way to do this is to say, "Let me be sure I understand what you just said," and repeat back what you heard. You'll be surprised how many times you haven't heard it correctly. It may be because you weren't listening, or it may be the person was not expressing himself clearly and didn't realize it until you repeated it back.

Here are some comical examples of how people sometimes express themselves unclearly. These are actual words taken from insurance company accident reports:

"I told the police I was not injured, but removing my hat, I found a skull fracture."

"I was thrown from my car as it left the road. I was later found in a ditch by some stray cows."

"The telephone pole was approaching fast. I attempted to swerve out of its path when it struck my front end."[29]

These statements probably brought some chuckles, but they are examples of how poorly people often communicate. We must choose our words carefully and verify with the listener what has been understood, especially when sending instructions or a message through a third party.

3: Don't let things fester.

When someone has said something that you didn't understand or with which you didn't agree or that hurt your feelings, don't let it brew inside of you. Go to that person as quickly as possible and talk it out.

If you've spoken to someone and you know you didn't communicate it the right way or you saw a puzzled look on his or her face, don't put off making it right. Molehills have a way of becoming mountains when anything is allowed to fester. Sometimes people will say they understand when they really don't because they are embarrassed to admit they either didn't hear you or didn't understand.

If something is bothering you or you sense someone else has a problem with what you have said, deal with it immediately. If you don't, all you're doing is letting the enemy gain a foothold. A wound that festers becomes infected and can become deadly.

Misunderstandings left to fester can destroy relationships. Be obedient to what the Bible says:

> When angry, do not sin; do not ever let your wrath (your exasperation, your fury or indignation) last until the sun goes down. Leave no [such] room or foothold for the devil [give no opportunity to him].
>
> Ephesians 4:26,27 AMP

4: What you don't say can have as much impact as what you do say.

You've probably heard the expression, "A picture is worth a thousand words." Well, facial expressions often say more than words can express. Body language, including facial expressions, is another way of communicating without words. It's all in the way you roll your eyes, raise an eyebrow, give "the look," sit, stand, hold your arms, or walk that tells people what you are feeling or even thinking.

When Joe Onosai, who is now one of our assistant pastors, first started coming to our church, he sat with his dark sunglasses on and wouldn't smile for anybody or anything. When people went up and tried to shake his hand, he simply crossed his arms; and when he did, his muscles got bigger. His facial expressions and body language said loud and clear, "Leave me alone!" He had an "attitude"! Since he rededicated his life to the Lord, he has become a great communicator and works very effectively with our youth. His face now shines with love and life.

When I get really focused and I'm thinking, I make certain facial expressions. I did this sometimes while sitting on the platform before the teaching started. Kuna would see me and think I didn't like the song or that something was wrong with praise and worship. Driving home she would ask, "Why did you do that?"

"Why did I do what?"

"That. That face. Art, you've got to stop making those faces. You're bothering people up there."

"I didn't do anything. I was in the Holy Ghost. What are you talking about?"

I had to become aware of what message I was transmitting by my facial expressions.

Let me share some facts with you about communication. When we communicate, we express feelings and attitudes through verbal skills and visual (non-verbal) skills. Verbal skills are the words we choose and the tone of voice we use. Visual (non-verbal) skills are facial expressions, such as a smile, a frown, a furrowed brow, and body language such as eye contact. Gestures are the way we use our hands. Posture is the way we stand, walk, or sit; and appearance includes grooming, what we wear, and the way we carry ourselves.

Dr. Albert Mahrabian, who holds a Ph.D. in Communication from UCLA, says that we communicate 7 percent by words, 38 percent by tone of voice, and 55 percent through visual (non-verbal) skills. The way in which we gather information is 87 percent by sight, 7 percent by hearing, 3.5 percent by smell, 1.5 percent by touch, and 1 percent by taste. This tells us how important what someone sees when we are talking to them is. Listeners need visual stimulation—a point of activity on which to focus. Therefore, it is important to use body language as a positive incentive to listen versus as a distraction.[30]

Suppose I'm in front of the congregation teaching on an important subject. I haven't slept very well the night before and I keep yawning during the presentation. I want to get this over with so I can go take my Sunday nap, and I'm pacing back and forth across the platform. At the same time, I have a nervous habit of jingling the change in my pocket. Do you think my message will hold people's attention? Probably not. Some will have fallen asleep from watching me yawn, some will have whiplash from watching me tread back and forth, and others will be wondering just how much money is in that pocket. Their focus will be on my body language and not on what I am saying.

Examine the facial expressions and body language you have allowed to creep into your communication. You may not be aware of your own habits and may need to ask someone close to you to honestly give you some constructive feedback. Another suggestion is to place a mirror and a tape recorder next to the telephone. Watch yourself in the mirror as you talk and tape your side of the conversation. You'll be surprised what you see in your facial expressions and hear in your voice. As you become aware of how you communicate, do what it takes to eliminate any bad habits that may be causing misunderstandings and sending the wrong signals. Remember, when you have a smile on your face, you have a smile in your voice.

5: It's not always what we say; it's what we allow others to say.

Some of us are so black and white, when we get in a conversation, we make our point and that's it—end of discussion. Believe me, I can tell you from experience that is not the way to encourage communication. Often we will learn more about life and about those around us when we allow others to do the talking while we do the listening.

One of the greatest experiences of my life has been letting my wife speak to me. She has helped me understand marriage and the woman I married by sharing her heart with me. As I shared earlier, this was an eye-opener for me because good communication skills were not strong points in my childhood training. I don't like details. Give me the headlines and let's get on with things. However, Kuna loves to elaborate and tells great stories. She doesn't leave out *any* of the details. I learned that if I want to relate to my wife, I have to be patient and get the amplified version of the headline. I have to listen to her, and by doing that she is edified and knows I care. I found out when I started really listening to what she was saying that she truly had something to say.

Our fast-paced American culture does not stimulate good listening skills. Everything is moving faster and faster. No one wants to wait more than a few seconds for a computer to boot up; and, heaven forbid, if someone hesitates turning a corner in a line of traffic. Fax machines, email, and answering machines have eliminated much of our verbal conversation and human contact. Television has reduced the average person's attention span to less than seven minutes. Psychologist John Rosemond says, "A child watching television isn't paying attention to any one image longer than three or four seconds. With routine exposure of that sort, it is hardly far-fetched to suppose that the attention span of a child would be compromised. With televisions in almost every household, you end up with an epidemic of kids...who are impulsive, disorganized and forgetful."[31]

Does that sound like anyone you know? Developing effective communication skills takes time and the benefits far outweigh the effort.

KEYS TO LISTENING

Real hearing is *honest* listening. Let's explore five keys to "real" hearing.

Key 1: Real hearing is stopping whatever you are doing and looking directly at the person who is speaking to you. It's not looking over his or her shoulder at who else might be in the room or at the television or at the papers on your desk in front of you or at the book or newspaper you're reading. If there are distractions in the room, move to another room and sit facing the person or persons to whom you are talking.

Key 2: Real hearing is listening to what the person is saying instead of thinking of what you're going to say next. In the earlier days of our marriage, whenever Kuna was trying to tell me something, I tried to jump ahead of what she was saying or interrupt and say, "Let me just make my point first."

In exasperation, she would say, "Art! You weren't listening to me, were you?"

My response often sparked an argument and neither one of us heard the other's point.

The average person speaks at about 150 words per minute. The average person thinks at approximately 600 words per minute—four times faster.[32] This is why our minds so easily wander from what the person is saying to us. The listener must focus completely on what the speaker is saying. Don't hesitate to take the time "after" the speaker finishes talking to gather your thoughts carefully before you respond.

Key 3: Real hearing is making eye contact with the person who is talking to you. It develops trust. Just like people reach out and clasp hands when they are introduced, it is important to "clasp" eyes when you begin a conversation. Hold that "clasp" for 3-5 seconds and then look randomly away. Staring without a break is uncomfortable for everyone. Three seconds may seem like a lifetime but you don't want to appear "shifty-eyed." Keep going back and making eye "clasps" throughout the conversation to show that you are interested and involved in what is being said.[33]

Key 4: Real hearing is being attentive. Create the impression that this conversation is important to you and that you value the message and the messenger. Don't let timidity or shyness be used as an excuse. Remember, your facial expressions will set the mood for the conversation. Sit up and lean forward slightly to show you are listening. Nod your head or interject a thought occasionally. Ask questions at an appropriate time and always let the speaker finish his or her thought before interrupting.

Key 5: Real hearing is less about speaking and more about listening to understand. The goal of any conversation is to connect, not defeat the other person or persons. Don't try to hit "hot buttons" that will cause conflict. The point is not having to be right all the time. Try to feel what the speaker is feeling. Jesus was a Man of compassion. Ask yourself, "What would Jesus say or do in this situation?" Speak truth in love. Someone once said, "Talking is sharing, but listening is caring."

In his book *Courtship After Marriage,* Zig Ziglar shares this story of a couple who had just celebrated their 50th wedding anniversary with their family and the entire community. It was late in the evening when they returned home and were finally alone.

> "As was his custom, the husband went to the kitchen, prepared a piece of toast and a small glass of milk, and called his wife to announce that it was ready. She walked into the kitchen, took one look at the snack and burst into tears. The husband was naturally puzzled and concerned, so he embraced her and asked what the problem was. She tearfully explained that she had thought that on this most special of all days he would have been more thoughtful and not given her the end piece of bread. The man was silent for a moment, and then he quietly said, 'Why, Honey, that's my favorite piece of bread.'

> "The irony is that for all those years he had been giving her what he considered to be the best, and she had been accepting it with the feeling that it was the worst."[34]

How many of us have experienced such disappointments and pain in life because we haven't been able to communicate at the simplest, everyday level?

Much of what we have been talking about in this chapter revolves around hearing and communicating with people. However, we must not leave out the most important relationship of all—the one we have with our heavenly Father and how we communicate with Him.

IT'S GOD TALKING

Have you ever been talking on the phone and suddenly realized the connection has been interrupted? Did you just shrug your shoulders and continue what you were saying? Of course not. More than likely, you felt rather foolish and wondered how long you had been talking to yourself. To experience the joy of living out God's plan and destiny to its fullest, each believer must have a meaningful relationship with God, which can only be accomplished through two-way communication with Him. Too many believers have one-sided conversations with God telling Him all of their wants and desires, crying about their problems and circumstances but not giving Him a chance to talk back to them. Sometimes they are afraid to hear what He might want to say to them; but most often, they just don't believe they can hear from Him so they don't even try to listen. It's like they are talking into a disconnected telephone.

God does talk back to us if we will just stop and listen. Sometimes He speaks through a passage of Scripture we are reading. Have you ever had a verse just jump off the page at you or suddenly understand something about a familiar verse you've never seen in it before? It is God talking. Other times the Holy Spirit drops a "knowing" about something in our spirit as He talks to us Spirit-to-spirit. There are even a few people who have actually heard the audible voice of God.

OPEN THE EAR GATE

Christians are notorious for hearing things and also for not hearing what they hear. That sounds like a contradiction, but it's not. We are notorious for not hearing what we hear because we are hearing with the outer ear, so we don't hear what God is saying. God will answer any question we ask and speak into our lives about important issues if we will listen with our "ear gate." This "ear gate" is an access door into your heart that allows you to understand what God is saying to you. So, if you want to hear from God, keep your heart open.

God created us to commune, or communicate, with Him and to speak into each other's lives. The level on which we were once able to communicate with Him was taken away and enmity came between God and humankind in the Garden of Eden when Adam and Eve disobeyed. That ability to communicate directly with Him was restored by Jesus on the cross. When Jesus returned to the Father, He left the Holy Spirit here on earth to comfort us and to teach us how to commune—communicate—with God at the level He originally intended. Jesus also provided the pattern for us to live in peace and harmony with each other. It is up to us to speak and to listen to Him and to each other in a godly manner to appropriate the blessings of good communication as it says in this Scripture:

A word fitly spoken is like apples of gold in settings of silver.

Proverbs 25:11

TAKE ACTION TODAY

1) What disappointments or miscommunication can you identify in your life similar to the story of the husband giving his wife his crust of bread?

2) What will you do to avoid such miscommunication in the future?

3) What steps will you take to be a better listener?

4) What communication weaknesses did you see in yourself as you read this chapter?

5) How will you turn these weaknesses into strengths in the next 30 days?

Chapter 5

{ Evaluate and Eliminate What Must Not Dominate }

"Lack of direction, not lack of time, is the problem.
We all have twenty-four hour days."[35]

Zig Ziglar

If each hour of the day is a treasure chest of opportunity, how much treasure did you accumulate in each hourly "chest" yesterday? How many opportunities passed you by because your time was consumed with busyness rather than the business of the day? To move from where you are to where you need to be—living out your God-given vision—you must evaluate and eliminate what must not dominate.

DETERMINE YOUR VALUES

As you considered your day yesterday, you may have thought, *I didn't accomplish all I would have liked to do, but I did some good things.* Let's see what the Bible says about some of those "good" things we do.

All things are lawful for me, but not all things are helpful;
all things are lawful for me, but not all things edify.

1 Corinthians 10:23

Now ask yourself, "Were the things I did helpful in reaching my goals and did they build me up?" The word *edify* means to "build up" or to increase.[36] All of the things going on in your life are not helpful or edifying to get you to the next level in God's plan for your life.

The word *evaluate* means "to determine or fix the value of or to determine the significance or worth of something by careful appraisal and study."[37] Just by dissecting the word itself, e-VALU-ate, we see "value" is the root of it. To eliminate the things that may be lawful but are not helpful or edifying, you must determine what "values" you have allowed to dominate your life that truly don't have value, virtue, or vision in them. In other words, you must weed out certain elements of your life that eat up your time, resources, energy, and effort but don't lend purpose or strength to your vision.

What we are talking about is the difference between a "good" thing and a "God" thing. A "good" thing is something we like and by which we derive pleasure and comfort. A "God" thing is His best for us and often it is harder to obtain or maintain. Reading a Christian novel is a "good" way to spend your time, but if it takes the place of your daily Bible study or if it robs you of a good night's sleep because you stay up half the night reading, then it may need to be eliminated or prioritized more appropriately. Anything that distracts you or causes you to stumble along the road to getting where you need to be is suspect.

ARE YOU IN SLAVERY?

The Message Bible gives us an interesting perspective on this from another Scripture verse.

> Just because something is technically legal doesn't mean that
> it's spiritually appropriate. If I went around doing whatever I
> thought I could get by with, I'd be a slave to my whims.

1 Corinthians 6:12 MESSAGE

Some people become slaves to every whim and fancy that comes along because they have no direction or purpose in life. Any new idea or "get rich quick" scheme or wind of doctrine that comes along draws them like a dog to a new bone.

If you find yourself going this way one day and that way the next but never getting anywhere, ask yourself what you need to eliminate to regain your focus. Don't allow yourself to be caught up with being extremely busy while under the power of minor things. Don't waste your life running after "good" things rather than focusing on "God" things. Keep continually evaluating and eliminating whatever distracts you from your vision and goals.

Now let's read the same Scripture in *The Living Bible*.

> I can do anything I want to if Christ has not said no, but
> some of these things aren't good for me. Even if I am
> allowed to do them, I'll refuse to if I think that they might
> get such a grip on me that I can't easily stop when I want to.

1 Corinthians 6:12 TLB

DISCIPLINE DAILY HABITS

Little daily habits can easily turn into bondage if we aren't careful. How many of us can't get our day started without our morning coffee? It seems innocent enough until the doctor tells one of us to eliminate all the caffeine in our diet, and we try getting along without our coffee.

I heard Rev. Kenneth Hagin tell this story in one of his meetings. He said, "I drink a lot of tea, and it occurred to me I'm being controlled by this tea. So, I'm going to fast from this tea for a while and just put it aside." He didn't have to do this, but he was taking care of a little fox that had crept into his daily routine. He was disciplining himself.

Discipline is a word that has gotten a bad rap. Some people have made it a long cuss word, but it's not. It takes discipline to stay focused and on track to where God is taking us in life. Without it, we begin tolerating bad habits, and before we know it, those habits begin dominating our lives. Here is what the Word says about discipline:

> For the time being no discipline brings joy, but seems
> grievous and painful; but afterwards it yields a peaceable
> fruit of righteousness to those who have been trained by it.
>
> Hebrews 12:11 AMP

WHAT DO YOU TOLERATE?

Whatever dominates you ultimately starts with what you have tolerated. Some of us have tolerated certain little things we knew weren't right, but we procrastinated and didn't deal with them. Now they are dominating major portions of our time, and we don't know how to stop it. This can happen in many areas of life.

Let's use television as an example. Television itself is not wrong. It doesn't have a mind of its own, and it doesn't tell you what to watch. You choose what you watch and how much you watch. You are the one who pushes the buttons on the remote control. Now the question is, how many hours of television do you watch a day in comparison with the amount of time you spend studying the Bible or interacting with your family? You may say, "Well, I'm getting rid of this television." The problem is not the television. You are the problem. You have tolerated watching more and more television until it has dominated your life. If getting rid of the television is the only way to eliminate the distraction, then so be it. Just make sure you understand that the real problem is a lack of self-discipline.

Suppose you tolerate not having a consistent prayer life or a consistent time for studying the Bible. Or, perhaps you tolerate going to church and don't enter into the praise and worship because you don't feel you have to participate. In actuality, you aren't receiving the benefits of all those elements that are meant to edify, strengthen, and build you up. Before long you find yourself getting bored and starting to think that something is wrong with the church or with the praise and worship team or with the pastor. It is none of these. You are the problem because you have tolerated being lukewarm. It is easier to blame someone else because that way you don't have to take responsibility for your own life.

GET RID OF UNNECESSARY WEIGHTS

It's time to get rid of the unnecessary weights we are carrying around that hinder our progress as this Scripture tells us:

Therefore we also, since we are surrounded by so great a
cloud of witnesses, let us lay aside every weight, and the sin
which so easily ensnares us, and let us run with endurance
the race that is set before us.

Hebrews 12:1

How many weights does it say to lay aside? *Every* weight. It
is time to evaluate what weights you are carrying. If you don't
evaluate your life from time to time, you'll never find out what is
holding you back. *The Message Bible* calls these weights "spiritual
fat." None of us need any extra fat, physical or spiritual.

Do you see what this means—all these pioneers who blazed
the way, all these veterans cheering us on? It means we'd
better get on with it. Strip down, start running—and never
quit! No extra spiritual fat, no parasitic sins.

Hebrews 12:1 MESSAGE

What is it that is keeping you from *living* the Word? In what
ways have you just been "going through the motions" in your spiritual walk? What is it that trips you up every time you determine in
your heart that you're going to have a regular time of prayer and
Bible study each day? It may even be a person or a group of people
who are weighing you down and monopolizing your time and
energy. It's time to examine those 24 treasure chests (hours) in
your day to identify the spiritual fat and get rid of it.

GOOD IS THE ENEMY OF BEST

Ninety-five percent of achieving anything is recognizing what
you don't want and eliminating what you don't need. Good is the

enemy of best, and a good thing is the enemy of a God thing. It's time to get rid of the "pack rat" mentality that hangs on to our boxes of "good" stuff in case we might need them sometime. We all know that "sometime" never comes. William Jones once said, "The art of being wise is the art of knowing what to overlook."[38]

God gave each of us different giftings so we can fulfill a specific purpose. He doesn't expect us to fulfill everyone else's calling, just our own. Often we try to be all things to all people and dabble in everything that comes our way. As a result, we become a "wandering generality" without focus or purpose. We must learn how to discern on what to focus our time, energy, and resources and what to overlook.

ESTABLISH YOUR FOCUS

The Pareto Principle states, "20 percent of your priorities will give you 80 percent of your production if you spend your time, energy, money and focus on the top 20 percent."[39] If you don't learn to organize your life, you're going to agonize over life. Examine how much time you are spending on things—people, habits, idiosyncrasies—that really aren't producing in your life what needs to be produced. You may even discover it is necessary to eliminate a few "good" things to get where you need to be.

In John 15, Jesus told us about the need to prune a tree in order to get more fruit. The branches that were pruned were alive, had leaves on them, and had produced fruit at one time. But in order for the tree to be more productive those branches had to be trimmed.

Every branch in Me that does not bear fruit He takes away;
and every branch that bears fruit He prunes, that it may bear
more fruit.

John 15:2

PRUNE THE TREE

If you want more fruit in your life, you're going to have to
prune the tree and remove those branches that are hindering a
higher level of productivity in your life. The tree may look barren
and ugly for a while, but only until the next growing season. You
may feel a sense of loss or be uncomfortable for a period of time
when you first eliminate these branches—weights or spiritual
fat—but as your life becomes more productive and your destiny
begins to unfold, you will rejoice in your new growing season.

LET PEACE RULE

As you evaluate what needs to be eliminated in your life,
allow the peace of God to be your umpire. Seek the will of God
and don't be led astray by the testimonies you hear from other
people. Just because everyone else is profiting from something
doesn't mean God wants you involved. You must be led by the
Spirit of God and not by the lust of the flesh. Stop being so competitive with one another and don't covet what others have. If you
follow God's plan in your life and follow the leadership of the
Holy Ghost, God will bless you.

My wife and I have a house that we love and enjoy because
we obeyed the voice of the Holy Ghost. When God told me to sell
our last house, real estate prices were in a slump. My Christian

realtor at the time told me it was a bad time to sell and not to do it. I was led by the Holy Ghost to ask a specific price for it, and I said to my realtor, "This is the amount God said to ask."

The realtor responded by saying, "You'll never get that kind of money. Nobody's asking for that kind of money in this neighborhood."

In two weeks, the house sold for the amount of money I had asked. God had to fly in someone from a foreign country to buy it, but God is not limited. He will do whatever it takes to prosper us when we are obedient to His voice.

KEEP PRIORITIES IN ORDER

We have 24 hours in each day. God wants us to be wise in choosing how to establish our priorities. Here's a story I've heard that illustrates how some of us lead our lives.

A lighthouse keeper, who worked on a rocky stretch of coastline, received his new supply of oil once a month to keep the light burning. Not being far from shore, he had frequent guests.

One night, a woman from the village begged him for some oil to keep her family warm. Another time, a father asked for some oil for his lamp to light his way back home. Another friend needed some oil to lubricate a squeaky wheel. Since all the requests seemed legitimate, the lighthouse keeper tried to please everyone and to grant all the requests that came across his path.

Toward the end of the month, he noticed that his supply of oil was very low. Soon, it was all gone and the beacon went out.

That night several ships were wrecked and lives were lost. When the authorities investigated, the lighthouse keeper was very repentant. To his excuses and pleading, their reply was, "You were given oil for one purpose, to keep the light burning!"

You've been given enough oil for a 24-hour day to fulfill God's purpose in your life. How much oil are you giving away to others trying to please them? If you don't focus your priorities and use your oil wisely, you may run out before you have completed your assigned tasks. It may be the difference between life and death for those divine appointments God has for you.

LINK PRIORITIES TO GOALS

Take time to sit down and examine your priorities and how you are spending your time. Your priorities should be directly linked to your vision and goals that you prepared in Chapter one. Robert J. McKain said, "The reason most major goals are not achieved is that we spend too much of our time doing second things first."[40] We have to learn to put first things first and don't make the mistake of thinking God is a second thing. Make Him first. Remember, "there is never a right time to do the wrong thing."[41] Be sure to include the Lord in this process every step of the way. Let the Holy Spirit be your guide.

FOCUS ON TWENTY PERCENT

Keep in mind that too many priorities will paralyze you. Focus in on the 20 percent that will give you 80 percent of your productivity. What are the important few priorities that are vital for you to meet your goals and fulfill your vision? Once you narrow down your top 20 percent, make a master list of your priorities and categorize them in order of importance with "urgent" being what needs to be done within the next 24-48 hours, "important" being things that need to be done within the next 3-5 days, and "necessary" being things that need to be completed within the next 6-14 days. It's a good idea to update your list on a weekly basis.

CHOOSE OR LOSE

As you categorize your list, you will begin to see what things need to be eliminated. It may surprise you how many things aren't as important as you thought they were. Decide what to do and do it. If you have a hard time eliminating good things in your life, say this to yourself, "Choose or lose!" If you don't choose to eliminate the "good" things, you will lose out on God's best. Be sure to consider what things you may need to delegate to someone else to do. God did not mean for us to work alone. Even the Lone Ranger had Tonto.

Make a daily "to do" list with no more than six items on it. Pick items from each of the three categories (urgent, important, and necessary) on your master list. Be realistic what your day will allow you to accomplish. In other words, if you know you are going to be tied up in a meeting for four hours, don't put more on your "to do" list than you can possibly finish. It will only frustrate you not to have accomplished your list.

SMALL BITES ADD UP TO A WHOLE

As you organize your day, concentrate on the urgent matters first, then the important, and then the necessary, but learn to use your time wisely. If you have a 15-minute block of time between meetings or before you need to pick up the kids at school, don't allow yourself to always pick the easier or less important tasks over the more urgent. Even urgent tasks can be broken down into bite-sized pieces of time. As you progress down your list, make note of what you have done and check off each item completed. When you plan the use of your time and prioritize your tasks, you will be amazed at how much more you can accomplish.

Whenever new opportunities come your way, ask yourself, "How does this fit into my top priorities/projects?" Seek wisdom from the Lord and be led by the promptings of the Holy Spirit whether it is appropriate to add it to your master list of priorities. Examine whether it is a "good" thing or a "God" thing. If it doesn't fit into your top 20 priorities, either eliminate it or set it aside for consideration at another time. God's timing is always perfect. Too often we learn too late what is *really* important.

X-OUT LIMITING ASSOCIATIONS

Increase and decrease come by association. We become like those with whom we associate. It's a spiritual law as this Scripture tells us:

> A mirror reflects a man's face, but what he is really like is shown by the kind of friends he chooses.
>
> Proverbs 27:19 TLB

That's pretty straightforward, isn't it? Here is more clearly stated truth regarding our associations:

> He who walks with wise men will be wise, but the companion of fools will be destroyed.
>
> Proverbs 13:20

As hard as this sounds, it is better to be alone than to be with the wrong company. I came across a newspaper article about a local elementary school dealing with a skunk problem. Skunks had been living and releasing odors near a drainage system next to one of the classroom complexes and the heating ventilation system had been carrying the odor to other parts of the building. When teachers and students began to complain about having headaches and problems concentrating, skunk traps were set, but to no avail. The school had to eventually hire a professional to take care of the skunk problem.

DON'T JOIN THE STINK POSSE

Skunk invasion is a problem that can appear not only with those pesky black and white creatures but also with negative and critical associates—friends, coworkers, and even family. Sometimes these stinky varmints sneak up on us, and we get so used to the odor we don't realize how it is affecting us. Are there any people close to you who have been causing you headaches, loss of concentration, missed opportunities, and a lack of success?

If a problem associate is stinking up your life, you have three options:

1) Choose to continue the relationship.

2) Try to change the conditions it produces.

3) Separate yourself from the source of the problem.

No relationship is neutral. If you choose to continue a "stinking" relationship, be prepared for the negative results it may bring to your life, because those who do not bring increase into your life inevitably will bring decrease. Associating with people who are angry, critical, negative, immoral, or ungodly will set a trap to draw you into their evil ways.

> Make no friendship with an angry man, and with a furious man do not go, lest you learn his ways and set a snare for your soul.
>
> Proverbs 22:24,25

RELATIONSHIPS SHAPE CHARACTER

Those with whom we spend the majority of our time shape our character. The old adage, "One bad apple spoils the barrel," is true in relationships as well as in storing fruit. Dr. Ed Cole, pastor, author, evangelist, and father of the Christian men's movement, once said, "You can tell the character of a man by the friends he keeps."[42] If you want to be a winner, you have to hang around people willing to win.

We must learn the power of right associations and the pitfalls of wrong associations. Right associations are important because they lift you up and advance you. When you surround yourself with the right kind of people, you enter into God-ordained power and agreement. Two people who are walking uprightly with the Lord form a threefold cord that is not easily broken.

> Two are better than one, because they have a good reward for their labor. For if they fall, one will lift up his companion...if two lie down together, they will keep warm...Though one

may be overpowered by another, two can withstand him. And a threefold cord is not quickly broken.

Ecclesiastes 4:9-12

As I look back at my life, every advancement I made was connected to a person—schoolteacher, soccer coach, friend. Each person had a desire to reach out to me and a relationship was made because these people took time and had a genuine care and concern for me. These were people who put their lives on hold to embrace and walk me through my early church life, who prayed for me, and who made a pivotal impact in my life.

I can recall, in particular, a friend who had a tremendous impact in my life during my college days at USC. Michael was a sold-out, committed Christian. We were both in the school of architecture and spent numerous hours studying and working on projects together. What amazed me about him was his conviction for Christ and his love for people.

We spent one summer in Venice, Italy, studying architectural design with some other students. At that time, I was totally unsaved. Michael always looked for opportunities to share the Gospel with me. He never condemned my buddies and me for our ungodly lifestyle, but rather he readily shared with us who Christ was in a real and meaningful way. Some nights when we were getting ready to go out to enjoy the Venice nightlife, he asked us if we would like to hear a story. Although we weren't really interested in being Christians at that time, we intently listened to those stories he read from the Bible because he made them sound so real and amazingly relevant to us.

Occasionally Michael asked me if I was ready to make a decision for Christ. He is not the one who led me to the Lord, but the good seed Michael took time to plant in me took root and resulted in transforming my life for eternity. For that I am eternally grateful.

SEEK WISE COUNSEL

As you seek God's direction regarding your relationships, His wisdom enters into your heart and disconnects you from wrong relationships. The Holy Spirit will prick your heart and let you know who fits into any of the categories mentioned in this Scripture:

> For wisdom and truth will enter the very center of your
> being, filling your life with joy. You will be given the sense
> to stay away from evil men who want you to be their
> partners in crime—men who turn from God's way to walk
> down dark and evil paths, and exult in doing wrong, for they
> thoroughly enjoy their sins.
>
> Proverbs 2:10-13 TLB

CHOOSE WISELY

The principles being presented for eliminating wrong relationships applies to people with whom you *choose* to associate. You can't choose your family, though you may be able to limit the amount of time you spend with extended family members or guard the way in which you allow immediate family members to influence your attitude. You may not be able to avoid certain people at work, but you can choose whether to hang around them during breaks, at lunch, or outside of work. It is the same for people at church because there are negative people in the church as well. The one group you can definitely choose is your friends, and you must carefully guard your heart because they can deeply impact your life. Emotional ties are difficult to break, but it may be necessary to do.

This story illustrates the importance of choosing friends wisely. "Two friends went backpacking into the wilderness. They woke up one morning and were standing next to their tent having their first cup of coffee. Suddenly, they spotted a grizzly bear heading toward them at full speed. Instantly, one man reached down, grabbed his tennis shoes, and quickly started to put them on. The other guy looked at him and said, 'Are you crazy? What are you doing? Do you really think you can outrun that grizzly bear?' His so-called friend said, 'No, I don't need to. All I have to do is outrun you!'"[43]

EVIL TRIUMPHS OVER GOOD

In every relationship, somebody is going to influence somebody. It is a fact that evil company triumphs over good. Perhaps not immediately, but in time evil company has a way of wearing down the good—like a wave continually washing upon the rocks until they are ground into sand. The Bible confirms this in 1 Corinthians 15:33. Let's look at this verse in three different Bible versions:

Do not be deceived: "Evil company corrupts good habits."

NKJV

Do not be misled: "Bad company corrupts good character."

NIV

Do not be deceived: "Bad company corrupts good morals."

NAS

THREE LEVELS OF RELATIONSHIP

The word *company* in this Scripture is the Greek word *homilia*,[44] which has three meanings. The first is "companionship," someone with whom you associate. The second is "social intercourse," which relates to being around certain people on a regular basis. The third meaning, "communion," signifies a deeper emotional interaction as very close friends or perhaps a romantic involvement. Companionship, social intercourse, and communion describe influence on every level of relationship. This isn't just about best friends. It's talking about anyone with whom you have consistent or continual contact.[45]

DON'T BE UNEQUALLY YOKED

Now do you see why it is so important to choose your close companions carefully? They influence your habits, character, and morals. That is why we are not to be "unequally yoked with unbelievers." This doesn't just apply to marriage relationships as it is so often inferred. It is talking about believers and unbelievers not being closely connected in any level of relationship. I like the way *The Living Bible* explains this principle:

> Don't be teamed with those who do not love the Lord, for
> what do the people of God have in common with the people
> of sin? How can light live with darkness? And what

harmony can there be between Christ and the devil? How can a Christian be a partner with one who doesn't believe?

2 Corinthians 6:14,15 TLB

Further proof of how strongly peers influence each other is evidenced in a Family in America survey conducted by the Barna Research Group in 1992. This study reported that the greatest influence on children is from their friends and peers—33 percent—as compared with 30 percent from parents, 21 percent from the media, 13 percent from schools, and 1 percent from churches and government.[46]

We can draw some interesting conclusions from this when considering that parents are having less than one third the impact on their children than other sources. Could it be that the amount of time children spend with parents is in direct correlation to the amount of influence parents have? More recent studies indicate that parents are spending 30 percent less significant time with their children than five years ago.[47] It doesn't take a rocket scientist to figure out that if the Barna study was conducted today, the statistics might be even more startling. Associations, both personal and through the media, strongly influence American society as a whole.

FACE THE TURNING POINT FIRMLY

The choice to change close associations is a major turning point in your life. It requires you to be willing to stand on your own two feet and be firm in your beliefs and standards. People who aren't willing to go as far as you want to go in Christ may say, "What are you trying to do, be better than us?" If you see yourself as weak, feeble, and insecure, you will bow down to what everyone says; but if you are strong and seeking wisdom from God, you won't be intimidated by such words. God will show you how to distance yourself from wrong associations.

Be careful that you don't associate with "average" people just because they are less challenging, easy to point at with your finger, and safe to conquer in their weakness. Mike Murdock, Christian author and musician, says, "It is worth it to pay the price to stay in the presence of extraordinary people, because your best qualities will surface in their presence."[48]

RESPECT GOD'S PLAN

Don't be deceived into thinking that people who speak perverse words and don't want to live a moral, godly life don't affect you. If you believe that, what you're saying is that you're smarter than God! Another lie is thinking you are going to "reach" them by hanging around with them. There is a big difference between ministering to people and hanging out together. Love such people from a distance, pray for them, and stretch your hand out real far. You don't have to be aloof or use a "holier-than-thou" attitude with them. The point is to respect what God is endeavoring to do in your life and not let any ungodly influences hinder your walk.

If God uses people to advance your life, isn't it likely that the devil uses people to cause you to retreat and fall back? The Bible talks about wolves in sheep's clothing. Believe it or not, some of these wolves are in church every Sunday. They sneak in to pull you out of the fold and out of the kingdom of God. Sometimes they don't even realize the enemy is using them. They hinder you by being small thinkers, critical backbiters, and gossip spreaders. Have you every seen a young person who is sweet and kind get hooked up with a new friend who is critical and always talking badly about all the other kids? Most likely within a few months, the sweetness was replaced by negative gossip. The sweetness didn't replace the criticism, did it?

Mrs. Olson was the town gossip in the classic TV series "Little House on the Prairie." In one episode, her ruthlessly negative tongue turned the entire town of Walnut Grove against the loving, gentle Doc Baker who had selflessly served the townspeople for years. Mrs. Olson was the wolf in sheep's clothing in that TV show many times. She thoroughly enjoyed her sins and often pulled others in as partners in her evil ways.

LET JESUS BE YOUR STANDARD

It is important to understand the spirit and attitude of the individuals with whom you closely associate, because as John Maxwell said, "Those closest to you will determine the level of your success."[49] When you associate with people who have the right attitude and spirit, your life becomes a reflection of them. Look what happens when you associate with Jesus! Your life reflects His love and compassion. Let Jesus and His Word be your standard for living. Then you can say to those around you, "I have this standard in my life, and if you're going to be around me, this is what I expect." When you set the standard and stand firm in it, others around you will either follow or go their own way.

If someone diverges from your standard, you may need to take this one aside and say, "You know I care about you and your friendship means a great deal to me. There are some things that really concern me about our relationship that I feel may hold us back from being where God wants us to be." (Discuss the specifics in a clear, concise, yet loving manner, and offer suggestions as to what changes need to take place. Speak the truth in love without being judgmental or condemning.) It is your choice to decide whether you are willing to work through these issues. I will help in any way I can. I have shared with you the standards I have set for my life, and I can't allow you to keep me from my destiny."

That is the only way you can have a positive influence on others and protect yourself from the pitfalls of wrong associations.

I've seen unmarried couples with such differences separate for a season until one or both have worked on certain areas of their character. They knew it was the will of God for them to marry and were mature enough not to proceed until their hearts and lives were right. After working out the issues that needed to be addressed, they then married and have been a tremendous testimony to the kingdom of God.

I've seen other couples who didn't have the courage to confront the issues in advance go forward into marriage and meet disaster at every turn. Their excuse often is, "Well, I didn't want to hurt his feelings." No one wants to hurt another's feelings, but that isn't the point. Their God-given destiny is at stake.

God values relationships and He intended for us to strengthen one another; as it says in Proverbs 27:17 in *The Message Bible*, "You use steel to sharpen steel, and one friend sharpens another." It is important to have someone that can speak truth into your life and challenge you to strengthen your weaknesses, someone with whom you can open up and be real without fear of condemnation or criticism.

Well-known author, pastor, and teacher William Arthur Ward defined the true measure of a friend when he said, "A friend knows your weaknesses but shows you your strengths, fields your fears but fortifies your faith, sees your anxieties but frees your spirit, recognizes your disabilities but emphasizes your possibilities."[50]

Examine the relationships in your life and measure them against the Scriptures we have discussed in this chapter. Do they talk doubt and unbelief or do they live their faith? Do they talk about what God can't do or celebrate what He does do? Do they talk about what you can't be or encourage you to be all that you can be? Do they criticize and gossip or encourage and strengthen? Celebrate those friends who accentuate the positive. They are worth their weight in gold. Eliminate those who pull you down and hold you back.

Using your time wisely, eliminating habits and relationships that hinder your growth and progress, and focusing your priorities are major steps in fulfilling your destiny and living your life on purpose. It takes courage to face such changes, but God gives us the grace for the moment when it is needed. Do what it takes to evaluate and eliminate whatever the Holy Spirit leads you to do. Whatever action you take, do it with His love and compassion as you move into God's plan and purpose for your life. You are about to experience a greater level of freedom in your daily walk with Him.

TAKE ACTION TODAY

1) How do you fill up the 24 treasure chests (hours) of your day?

2) What values dominate your life?

3) What do you need to eliminate?

4) What daily habits do you need to discipline?

5) How will you link your priorities with your goals?

6) What relationships do you need to eliminate or change and how will you accomplish this?

Chapter 6

{ Never Allow Small Thinking To Master Your Big Dreams! }

"How you think determines what you become."[51]

Zig Ziglar

Small thinking settles for "average, status quo" living bound on four sides by the stagnant waters of mediocrity—on the north by compromise, on the south by indecision, on the east by past thinking, and on the west by lack of vision. An "average" lifestyle does not make room for fulfilling your greatest potential in Christ from whom you gain your strength and focus to guard against mediocrity. Small thinking must be shattered if you expect to live your life on purpose and master your big dreams.

The apostle Paul challenges us in numerous Scriptures to break through the glass ceiling of relying on human effort alone by embracing all that we are and can be *in* CHRIST.

I have strength for all things in Christ Who empowers me [I am ready for anything and equal to anything through Him Who infuses inner strength into me; I am self-sufficient in Christ's sufficiency].

Philippians 4:13 AMP

Him we preach and proclaim, warning and admonishing and instructing everyone...that we may present every person mature (full-grown, fully initiated, complete, and perfect) in Christ (the Anointed One). For this I labor [unto weariness], striving with all *superhuman energy* which He so mightily *enkindles and works within me.*

Colossians 1:28,29 AMP

To do this we must identify and change our small thinking so that we can live by the "unlimited" limits of the unlimited One—Christ Jesus. That involves a leaning of our "entire personality on God in Christ in absolute trust and confidence in His power, wisdom, and goodness..." (Heb. 6:12 AMP).

SURVIVE SUCCESS

Everyone has experienced the damaging effect of small thinking, or limitations, that hinder new levels of growth and accomplishment. One of the major hindrances that holds us back is not failure, as many would think, but becoming satisfied with success, either past or present. When things seem to be going well, it is real tempting to kick back and let life happen. The problem is that life is a progression. You are either moving forward or backward, but you are not standing still. Unchecked satisfaction robs you of your cutting edge, your hunger, your fire, and your desire to press on into all God has for you.

If you want to master your God-given dreams, you must learn how to survive success. The way to do this is by not allowing yourself to become so satisfied with what you have gained that it puts a fear in you of moving forward lest you lose what you have already attained. People operating in such fear may say, "Well, I've got more than I've ever had in my life; I'd better not push myself any further." Or, another phrase often heard is, "I'd better not push my luck!" Beware of this subtle tactic of the enemy to stop you in your tracks and prevent you from stepping out in faith to fulfill your dreams and goals.

REMEMBER WHAT MOTIVATES SUCCESS

Another key to surviving success is to remember the steps that motivated you to become the success that you know you are. Sometimes people get so caught up in enjoying the benefits of their success they forget how they got there.

Evangelist and author Jesse Duplantis says the definition of *blessed* is "to be highly favored and empowered to prosper, or succeed." God has given us the ability to prosper, but we must understand that each success is only one rung on the ladder to greater things God has for us to accomplish. He wants us to keep reaching forward as the apostle Paul said in this Scripture:

> Brethren, I do not count myself to have apprehended; but one thing I do, forgetting those things which are behind and reaching forward to those things which are ahead, I press toward the goal for the prize of the upward call of God in Christ Jesus.
>
> Philippians 3:13,14

BEWARE OF STATUS QUO MEDIOCRITY

The curse of our society has to be "status quo," "mediocrity." Millions of people have buried their latent talents, gifts, and abilities in the cemetery of their last accomplishment because they have settled for the "status quo." How many people do you know who are still holding onto their Little League trophies or who never stop talking about their college football years? Such past successes can become anchors holding them back from fulfilling their destiny.

God doesn't want anyone to live in the wilderness of "status quo." It wasn't God's idea for the children of Israel to wander in the wilderness. Remember, they turned a 14-day journey into 40 years because of their small thinking and disobedience.

Are you pressing forward to master your big dreams? Be careful that you aren't equating busyness with pressing on. Mediocrity is not based on activity but on your mentality. Paul is not talking about the physical act of reaching forward but rather a mindset. He is warning us not to make mediocrity the milestone of our accomplishments. Be aware of what you are measuring, because history makers and world shakers have never been status quo, mediocre, or average people. They are people who think big and live outside the box called "average."

EXAMINE PREVAILING THOUGHT PATTERNS

Sometimes we impose limitations on ourselves, and other times the limitations are placed on us by people around us. I grew up in a non-Christian household in southern California. My mother grew up working hard picking fruits and vegetables in the lemon groves and tomato fields. She had a strong work ethic, but she had experienced prejudice at every turn. She kept saying, "Don't expect much out of life because of your color, how you were brought up, and your cultural background, because this is California." These limitations had been ingrained in my parents, and they were reflected in the way we lived—poor.

Children are conditioned by the prevailing thought patterns of their family, and this was definitely a prevailing thought pattern in my family. My parents weren't trying to hurt me. They were simply expressing how life had been for them, and they didn't know of any other way to live. It was up to me to break this pattern of small thinking. I had a choice to either live by the "que sera sera" mentality—whatever will be will be—or to step into what God's will was for my life.

It was God's will for the children of Israel to go into the Promised Land, but the Israelites limited themselves with small thinking. Their prevailing thought pattern caused them to see themselves as grasshoppers, and they allowed it to override God's will. Joshua and Caleb were the only history makers in the group, and they saw the Promised Land flowing with milk and honey. They had the faith to go in and take the land. There are a lot of things God wills for His people that they don't step into because of fear and small thinking.

IMPACTING GENERATIONS

History reveals that individuals who impacted their generations and affected the world most dramatically were those who, because of circumstance, pressure, or adversity:

Challenged the tide of convention,

Stretched the boundaries of traditions,

Violated the expectations of "status quo,"

Upset the mind of "the average,"

Shattered the wit of "the norm" and

Broke through the accepted" in order to accomplish the unexpected.

Such people do that little extra that others thought could not be done. Each of us has the ability to impact our generation in just such a dramatic fashion because we have the strength, self-sufficiency, and anointing of the Anointed One dwelling inside us.

EXERCISE YOUR OPTIONS

Just as I had a choice of whether or not to accept my family's prevailing thought pattern or any other limitations in my life, you also have a free will to choose a different road. Don't think that because you've accepted Jesus into your life that you're on auto pilot. You have to make decisions.

Whether you choose to think small or live big is up to you.

It is a sad fact that only a select few will make the quality decision to maximize every fiber of their lives by fully using their gifts, talents, and abilities. The question is, "Will you choose to exercise your options?"

BURIED GOLD

Pastor, author, and evangelist Dr. Myles Monroe tells this significant story:

"The wealthiest spot on this planet is not the oil fields of Kuwait, Iraq or Saudi Arabia; neither is it the gold and diamond mines of South Africa, the uranium mines of the Soviet Union or the silver mines of Africa. Though it may surprise you, the richest deposits on our planet lie just a few blocks from your house. They rest in your local cemetery or graveyard.

"Buried beneath the soil within the walls of those sacred grounds are dreams that never came to pass, songs that were never sung, books that were never written, paintings that never filled a canvas, ideas that were never shared, visions that never became reality, inventions that were never designed, plans that never went beyond the drawing board of the mind and purposes that were never fulfilled. Our graveyards are filled with potential that remained potential."[52]

Have you been conditioned to think small? Is your potential being stifled by limitations? A young man tells this story about limitations:

"One summer as I was packing to spend three months with relatives at a lake up north, my dad asked me to take my goldfish with me, because he didn't want to take care of it all summer.

"The day after we got to the lake, I decided to become a liberator. I went down to the dock with my fish bowl and gave my fish a little talk. 'I'm going to throw you in this lake,' I said. 'You will be free. You can eat well here and grow up to be a big fish.' When

I put the goldfish in the water at the end of the dock, it stayed right there. I backed off, thinking the fish was attached to my shadow. But when I moved back to be sure it was gone, it was still right there. I even threw a stone into the water to scare it away, but that goldfish just swam around it.

"When I came back after lunch, the goldfish was still there, swimming in the same spot. I sat down and thought, *That fish should be free. It's got the whole lake to swim in.* Suddenly I saw a huge ripple in the water. Splash! A big bass swallowed my little goldfish.

"Later in life someone told me that a goldfish, once it has lived in a circumference of a certain size, has been conditioned to think small. It will stay there until it dies—swimming in that small circle."[53]

All too often, we find ourselves swimming in small circles like a goldfish when we have the whole ocean in which to swim and expand our potential. Kevin Baerg, an author, speaker, and seminar leader, said, "We all have the promise that life contains infinite possibilities...yet most of us settle for a routine that narrows our life to the dimensions of a prison cell."[54]

SIX WAYS TO OVERCOME SMALL THINKING

Here are six ways to overcome small thinking and master your big dreams.

1: Realize there is more to life than what you may have experienced.

God wants you to live a *big* life. His desire is for you to live triumphantly.

> For I know the thoughts that I think toward you, says the Lord, thoughts of peace and not of evil, to give you a future and a hope.
>
> Jeremiah 29:11

> The thief does not come except to steal, and to kill, and to destroy. I have come that they may have life, and that they may have it more abundantly,
>
> John 10:10

In order to live *big*, you must get rid of tunnel vision and look at life with peripheral vision. Tunnel vision is what a race-horse has when he is wearing blinders on his eyes. All he can see is straight ahead. He can't see the other horses beside him or the crowd in the stands. It's what some people call "having a one-track mind." It works for a racehorse that may be easily distracted, but it doesn't work for someone who needs to be able to see what is happening all around him.

Marcus Allen, one of the greatest football players of our time, often talked about his incredible peripheral vision. His range of vision was so broad, he could spot a player coming from any direction to block him or zero in on a hole in the defensive line and blast right on through. This kept him one step ahead of the opposition and allowed him to change direction quickly when needed because he didn't get boxed in.

Peripheral vision allows you to take advantage of opportunities in life that someone with tunnel vision would never see. It allows you to see what is waiting for you so you can live a wide-open, spacious life. Where you are right now is not all there is for you. God has a future and a hope prepared for you. It's up to you to shatter the small thinking mentality that has given you tunnel vision and put limitations on your life.

If you want something you've never had before, you're going to have to do something you've never done. Too many people are not unhappy enough to change anything about their unhappiness. They sit and complain about it but aren't dissatisfied enough to change what they are doing. They are unhappy with their marriage but aren't willing to take responsibility for their actions or do what it takes to correct what is wrong. Maybe they are unhappy about not having a job, but they aren't unhappy enough to go out and find a job. Many are unhappy with being overweight but not enough to discipline their eating habits and deny their desire for hot fudge sundaes. They have learned to tolerate mediocrity, the status quo.

You cannot become who you need to be by remaining who you are or where you are. You must identify and change your limited, small thinking by renewing your mind with the Word of God and acting on it.

2: God doesn't box you in, but it takes faith in God's Word to bust you out.

God's salvation does not have "limits." It is freely given. You can live by the unlimited boundaries of an unlimited God just as David, the psalmist, did.

> But I will hope continually, and will praise You yet more and more. My mouth shall tell of Your righteousness and Your salvation all the day, for I do not know their limits.
>
> Psalm 71:14,15

God and His Word are one and the same. His Word does not limit you. It opens you up and frees you.

> If you abide in My word, you are My disciples indeed. And you shall know the truth, and the truth shall make you free.
>
> John 8:31,32

If you don't have any Word in you, you don't have the ability to break out of your unhappiness. You must plant the Word inside of you for God's power to operate out of you. As a believer, you have the right to let go of worry, stress, fear, disease, sickness, depression, oppression, anxiety, and the lordship of the devil.

> He sent His word and healed them, and delivered them from their destructions.
>
> Psalm 107:20

Faith in God's Word makes you what you need to be—free! Without faith you are a prisoner, because the devil wants you to live in the "safe zone of unbelief." It is faith in God's Word that takes the blinders off your eyes and destroys tunnel vision. Be careful and don't swallow the lies of the devil.

> But even if our gospel is veiled, it is veiled to those who are perishing, whose minds the god of this age has blinded, who do not believe, lest the light of the gospel of the glory of Christ, who is the image of God, should shine on them.
>
> 2 Corinthians 4:3,4

Faith is the required ingredient for busting out of the box of limitations in which a person is living. Every man or woman who has experienced the power of God had to be in faith for something to happen. The great men and women of Hebrews 11 experienced God's promises by faith. God spoke to Noah to build an ark in a place where there was no water at a time when it had never rained on the earth. Noah believed it, lived it, and took action. Each of these Bible greats learned that without faith they could not please God or receive His rewards.

> But without faith it is impossible to please Him, for he who comes to God must believe that He is, and that He is a rewarder of those who diligently seek Him.
>
> Hebrews 11:6

Has anyone ever said to you, "I'll believe it when I see it?" What they are really saying is they don't believe it is possible unless they can see it. This story illustrates one man who had faith for his vision and another who wouldn't believe it because he couldn't see it.

"Walter asked his friend to go for a ride with him far out in the country. They drove off the main road and through groves of trees to a large, uninhabited expanse of land. A few horses were grazing, and a couple of old shacks remained. Walter stopped the car, got out, and started to describe with great vividness the wonderful things he was going to build. He wanted his friend, Arthur, to buy some of the land surrounding his project and get in on the ground floor. But Arthur thought to himself, *Who in the world is going to drive 25 miles for this crazy project? The logistics of the venture are staggering.*

"Walter explained to his friend, 'I can handle the main project myself, although it will take all of my money. But the land bordering it, where we're standing, in just a couple of years will be jammed with hotels, restaurants, and convention halls to accommodate the people who will come to spend their entire vacation here at my park.' He continued, 'I want you to have the first chance at this surrounding acreage, because in the next five years it will increase in value several hundred times.'

"'What could I say?' Arthur said, 'I knew he was wrong. I knew he had let a dream get the best of his common sense, so I mumbled something about a tight money situation and promised that I would look into the whole thing a little later on.'

"'Later will be too late,' Walter cautioned Arthur as they walked back to the car. 'You'd better move on it right now.'"

This was how Art Linkletter turned down the opportunity to buy up all the land that surrounded what was to become *Disneyland*. His friend, Walt Disney, tried to talk him into it, but Art was challenged by the circumstances and didn't have faith in what he couldn't see.[55]

Sensory-driven people are those who see in black and white. The Bible says they are carnally minded, seeing only those things seen with their natural eyes. To be in faith, a person must be spiritually minded—able to believe in what can't be seen because God's Word says it is true.

> Now faith is the substance of things hoped for, the evidence
> of things not seen.
>
> Hebrews 11:1

When we are bound up by circumstances—things we can see—we aren't walking by faith. We must walk by faith in order to appropriate God's promises in our lives. Take a few moments to reflect on this poem:

"Doubt sees the obstacles

Faith sees the way.

Doubt sees the darkest night

Faith sees the day.

Doubt dreads to take a step

Faith soars on high.

Doubt questions 'who believes?'

Faith answers, 'I.'"[56]

3: To change small living, you must start by changing small thinking.

"Small living" is not ultimately a condition of circumstances, but the unwillingness to change small thinking to God's thinking. What we don't realize is that such small thinking comes from within us. God does not want us living in smallness. He has *big* plans for us. The apostle Paul challenges us to live *big*.

> Dear, dear Corinthians, I can't tell you how much I long for
> you to enter this wide-open, spacious life. We didn't fence
> you in. The smallness you feel comes from within you. Your
> lives aren't small, but you're living them in a small way. I'm
> speaking as plainly as I can and with great affection. Open
> up your lives. Live openly and expansively!
>
> 2 Corinthians 6:11-13 MESSAGE

This Scripture is proof that you don't have to live a small,
defeated life. Small thinking doesn't come from God. It's our own
choices about how we feel about ourselves that cause us to feel
small. Eleanor Roosevelt once said, "No one can make you feel
inferior without your consent."[57] King Solomon addressed this
when he said, "For as he thinks in his heart, so is he" (Prov. 23:7).

Small thinking is the result of an unrenewed mind. The key
to changing small thinking is thinking big according to the greater
One who lives in you—Christ Jesus. Start washing your mind with
the Word of God on a daily basis and watch small thinking disappear. When you let God be God, you'll discover His ways are
better than yours. God works in you to do big things in the small
places of your life by renewing your mind to His thoughts through
the power of the Holy Spirit.

> So are My ways higher than your ways, and My thoughts
> than your thoughts...So shall My word be that goes forth
> from My mouth; it shall not return to Me void. But it shall
> accomplish what I please, and it shall prosper in the thing
> for which I sent it.
>
> Isaiah 55:9,11

Consider carefully these three warnings about small thinking:

Don't be brought under the power of small thinkers. "All things are lawful for me, but all things are not helpful. All things are lawful for me, but I will not be brought under the power of any" (1 Cor. 6:12).

Do not allow the smallness of others to get into you—guard your heart. "Keep your heart with all diligence, for out of it spring the issues of life" (Prov. 4:23).

Be careful what you deposit, because you will get a return—according to your faith be it unto you! "So then faith comes by hearing, and hearing by the word of God" (Rom. 10:17).

It's time to stop blaming circumstances, other people, or God for your small thinking. Make a decision today to change what is within you—your mindset. Only then can you really change the world around you.

4: Make the decision to live large.

Your life is not small. God has done no small thing in you. Start acting like who you are—in Christ—not who you "think" you are.

> You are of God, little children, and have overcome them,
> because He who is in you is greater than he who is in
> the world.
>
> 1 John 4:4

It's time to start living according to the image of God as His sons and daughters.

> Be strong in the Lord [be empowered through your union
> with Him]; draw you strength from Him [that strength
> which His boundless might provides].
>
> Ephesians 6:10 AMP

The key to living large is not to live by what the world says but by what the Word of God says. Start by agreeing with His words and speaking them into your life.

The world says:

"You can't; you won't."

"Why try; give up; be real."

"It's too late; it's never been done!"

The Word of God says:

I can do all things through Christ who strengthens me.

Philippians 4:13

Be strong in the Lord and in the power of His might.

Ephesians 6:10

In all these things we are more than conquerors through Him who loved us.

Romans 8:37

As He is, so are we in this world.

1 John 4:17

5: Determine to bust out.

You may be living life smaller than God designed your life to be lived and not yet realize it. Are you your greatest limiting factor? If so, resign from the job. It's time to take big steps on behalf of your big God by mixing your faith with the big promises of His Word. Choose to live according to this Scripture:

> That He would grant you, according to the riches of His glory, to be strengthened with might through His Spirit in the inner man, that Christ may dwell in your hearts through faith; that you, being rooted and grounded in love, may be able to comprehend with all the saints what is the width and length and depth and height—to know the love of Christ which passes knowledge; that you may be filled with all the fullness of God. Now to Him who is able to do exceedingly abundantly above all that we ask or think, according to the power that works in us.
>
> Ephesians 3:16-20

6: Dare to believe God—*live big!*

Don't be afraid to use what you have—potential! I define *potential* as dormant ability, reserved power, untapped strength, unused success, hidden talents, capped capability. It's all you can be but have not yet become, all you can do but have not yet done, how far you can reach but have not yet reached, what you can accomplish but have not yet accomplished. Potential is unexposed ability and latent power. Potential is, therefore, not what you have done (lived), but what you are yet able to do (live).

Start living a *big* life even though you may be living in a small place at the moment. Take your eyes off your past, because your past is not your potential. Choose to liberate your future. The way to start is by changing the treasure in your heart from the inside out, by taking one step at a time to overcome small living and small doing, and by taking control of your life by the Word of God! Never despise small beginnings and remember this: "It's never too late to be what you might have been."[58]

TAKE ACTION TODAY

1) What small thinking is holding you back from mastering your dreams?

2) In what ways have you become satisfied with success?

3) What motivates you to be a success?

4) What talents, gifts, or abilities have you buried in the cemetery of your last accomplishment?

5) What prevailing thought patterns of small thinking from your family have impacted your life?

6) What steps will you take in the next 21 days to break out of your "status quo, average" lifestyle?

Chapter 7

Exercise Your Own Ax

"No bird soars too high, if he soars
on his own wings."[59]
William Blake

Have you ever watched a skilled lumberjack cut down a large tree with an ax? It's somewhat of a lost art in this day of power chainsaws, but there are still a few "old timers" around who know how to wield an ax proficiently. It is quite a sight to see the powerful swing of a muscular man's arms and hear the rhythmic "whack" of the ax blade slice into the hard trunk of the tree, sending wood splinters flying in all directions. It is dangerous and energy sapping work if the required knowledge isn't applied and necessary preparations aren't made as the foolish young man in this story illustrates.

"One day in a Northwestern forest, a man came across a lone lumberjack. He watched for a while as the man feverishly worked to saw down a large tree.

"What are you doing?" the man asked.

"Can't you see?" came the impatient reply from the young lumberjack. "I'm sawing down this tree."

"You look exhausted," the old-timer said.
"How long have you been at this?" The young man
said, "Over five hours, and I'm beat! This is very
hard work."

"It looks as if your saw might be a bit dull," the
older man said, not yet ready to reveal that he had
more than thirty years of experience as a lumberjack.

"It probably is," he said. "I've been sawing
for hours."

"Why don't you take a break for a few minutes
and sharpen your saw?" the old lumberjack suggested.
"I'm sure your job would go a lot faster."

The young man said, "I don't like to sharpen.
And right now, I don't have time to sharpen. I'm too
busy sawing!"[60]

King Solomon must have been watching this young lumberjack work when he wrote this Scripture.

> Whoever splits logs may be endangered by them. If the ax is
> dull and its edge unsharpened, more strength is needed but
> skill will bring success.
>
> Ecclesiastes 10:9,10 NIV

How many times do we waste time and energy, just like this
young lumberjack, because we don't use a tool in the way it was
meant to be used or won't take the time to care properly for the
tool so it will work more effectively? Other times, we don't take
the time to learn how to use it correctly and stumble along by trial

and error. We do what we like to do and not what we ought to do. Then we grumble and complain because we are tired and can't seem to get the results we want from our efforts.

An ax is a tool designed for the specific purpose of cutting or chopping wood. The head of the ax is made of steel so it will withstand the punishment of continual impact with the hard wood, and so it can be ground to a sharp edge. Axes come in all sizes and weights to perform different functions. A large ax may be used for cutting down tall trees. A smaller ax, sometimes called a hatchet, may be used to chop firewood into small pieces of kindling for starting a campfire. One thing all axes have in common is that they must be kept sharp in order to do the job they are meant to do.

YOUR "AX" IS UNIQUE

God gives each one of us an "ax"—a gift, calling, or ability— to fulfill a purpose that serves Him, mankind, and us as individuals. Only you can use the "ax" He gives to you for the specific purpose He assigns to you. No one can do what you are designed to do. When God calls you, He also equips you naturally *and* spiritually with all the tools you need to do what He wants you to do.

My wife, Kuna's, "ax" is a beautiful singing voice and an anointing to lead praise and worship. There are many others who can sing and lead praise and worship, but none of them are anointed in *exactly* the same way as Kuna. She takes us from the valley, up to the mountaintop, and right on into the throne room of God.

The job of sharpening the ax lies with the one who holds it. Just as a lumberjack must sharpen his ax so it will make a clean cut in the wood, Kuna has sharpened her natural musical skills with training and continual practice. She has sharpened her spiritual skills by listening to the Holy Spirit in selecting the right songs for each service, praying and believing for the Holy Spirit to move upon the other musicians and the people in the congregation, and following the promptings of the Spirit during each service to accomplish what God desires to be done, even if it means moving in a different direction than she had planned.

This didn't take place overnight. It took years for her to sharpen her musical skills to get to where she is today. She couldn't do it in her own physical strength. She had to rely on the wisdom of God and had to learn how to flow in the anointing of the Holy Spirit in order to move a congregation from simply singing songs into praising the Lord and then into glorious worship.

DISCOVER YOUR "AX"

The "ax" God has for *you* must be discovered, developed, and dispensed by *you*. Start by taking time to discover what your "ax" is. It could be something you already do or it may be something God has called you to do that you have not yet done. The best way to discover your own "ax" is to ask yourself, "What gives me joy and excites me?" Whatever talent or gift dominates your thoughts and stimulates your energy to pursue it is a good indication of what your "ax" is. It may be that you love to sing or play an instrument. God may have birthed in you the heart of a psalmist or a praise and worship leader. Perhaps you like to be with children and help them learn how to play games and sports. Your "ax" may be a teaching gift to be a schoolteacher or a coach.

In searching for your own "ax," don't just look back at what you have done. Look forward to what you would like to do. Consider the deep God-given desires of your heart, no matter how impossible they may seem, and stand on His promises.

> Delight yourself also in the Lord, and He shall give you the desires of your heart. Commit your way to the Lord, trust also in Him, and He shall bring it to pass
>
> Psalm 37:4,5

Desire alone is not enough as this verse tells us. We must first "delight ourselves in the Lord." That means to come into His presence and enjoy a close relationship with Him. When we do that, He imparts His desires into our hearts. Then we must "commit our way to Him." That means to release us totally to His care and His will. Lastly, we must "trust in Him," rely on and be confident that He will do what He has promised.

BE AN ORIGINAL, NOT A COPY

Your "ax" is God's gift, and it is uniquely fitted to you. Pray and ask the Holy Spirit to reveal or confirm to you what your specific "ax," or gifting, is and where it fits in your generational purpose. We all have a purpose to be fulfilled in our time—the reason we were born to this generation. Don't be surprised to discover that your gifting falls in line with the dreams and vision you explored in the first chapter of this book. Your "ax" is the tool needed to bring your vision into reality—it's your potential.

In seeking to discover your own "ax," don't fall into the dangerous trap of looking at anyone else's "ax." You were born to be an original, not a copy. When you're trying to be like someone else, the best you can ever be is number two. You can't use someone else's "ax" to do what you are called to do. No one is better qualified to fulfill your destiny or vision than you are.

Have you ever seen a cow or a horse stretching its neck through the fence to eat grass when there is a huge green pasture inside the fence? That must be how God sees us—yearning for someone else's gifts or talents—when we try to copycat other people instead of being who He made us to be. I love the wisdom of this statement I've heard, "The grass may be greener on the other side of the fence, but there's probably more of it to mow."

It has been noted that we relinquish three-quarters of ourselves in order to be like other people. I believe it is better to fail an original than to succeed an imitation. When you pick up another man's "ax" and try to imitate him, you may be attempting to do something you have no ability to accomplish. There is no greater waste of time or energy than trying to display qualities you don't possess. Conformity to the wrong things can be stifling, because it is the jailer of innovation and the enemy of growth. Stop looking over the fence. Focus on discovering your own "ax."

PREPARE YOUR "AX" FOR GREATER USE

Take the time to prepare, or sharpen, your "ax" for greater use. Someone once said, "The will to win is not nearly as important as the will to prepare." A champion doesn't win a race by just showing up at the starting line. It takes months, if not years in advance, of painful, grueling preparation to bring home the gold.

In 1972 Bruce Jenner watched Nikolay Avilov of the USSR set a world record of 8,454 points in the decathlon competition. Bruce saw himself standing on the platform at the 1976 Olympic Games winning the gold medal.

For the next four years, he committed himself to that goal. Every decision was weighed against the question, "Will it increase my chances for winning the gold medal in the 1976 Olympic Games?"

When Bruce Jenner's moment came in 1976, he not only won the Gold but set a new world record—8,634 points. Bruce Jenner accepted no excuses, only results, from his years of preparation.[61]

If you want to experience all that God has for you to accomplish in life, you must make that sacrificial commitment to do whatever it takes to prepare and sharpen your "ax." It may mean going back to college or attending Bible school. It may mean setting aside a certain amount of time each week to study the Scriptures and feed your mind with the Word of God. You may have to make major changes in your lifestyle or geographical location. It won't be easy, but God will see you through if you are willing and faithful.

Remember, a house isn't built in a day, and you must not despise small beginnings. Your "ax" may be in its infant stage, and without proper preparation, it will never mature. If God has given you a big vision, He is going to require you to build a solid foundation before He allows you to erect the walls and put on the roof. Go the extra mile and pay the price to sharpen your "ax" during your time of preparation.

> [Put first things first.] Prepare your work outside and get it
> ready for yourself in the field; and afterward build your
> house and establish a home.
>
> Proverbs 24:27 AMP

Or,

> Develop your business first before building your house.
>
> Proverbs 24:27 TLB

I played soccer in high school but I soon realized if I wanted to compete, I had to improve my speed. I spent one summer running up and down the steps of the stadium at Santa Barbara City College where I lived. It was a grueling workout. When I first started training, every time I ran to the top of the stadium I got sick to my stomach. But I didn't stop running. I'd get mad at my body for being out of shape and my legs would burn like fire, but I kept working at it. I didn't have as much natural ability as some players, but I worked at developing the skill I did have. My efforts paid off. My game improved to a level that afforded me a soccer scholarship at USC and an invitation to play soccer as a member of a national team in Europe. It all started with a little desire, a little

EXERCISE YOUR OWN AX

extra effort, and discipline. But I didn't despise the small beginnings. You shouldn't either.

EXERCISE YOUR "AX"

Once you have discovered and developed your God-given "ax," it is up to you to exercise it and let the gift start flowing. Using an ax in the natural requires considerable practice and skill. You can't just reach down, pick up an ax, and chop down a tree. The first time you swing and hit that tree or log you'll feel like you hit a concrete wall. Even using a small hatchet is a challenge until you learn how and where to hit the chunk of wood to penetrate the grain of the wood. A good woodsman learns how to read a tree or a piece of wood to know exactly where and at what angle to bring the ax into contact with the wood to get a good cut. He makes it look easy, but it's not. It takes many swings to perfect any measure of skill. That's how it will be for you in learning how to exercise your "ax." You'll hit some hard places and make some mistakes, but with practice and experience, you will perfect the skill you need to fulfill your God-given destiny.

As you step into this stage in your spiritual development, let me advise you on two points.

1: Have confidence in your own "ax" and keep on sharpening it.

New York Yankee's pitcher Don Larson pitched the first no-hit, no-walk World Series "perfect" game in baseball history in 1956 against the Brooklyn Dodgers. He was considered the best-of-the-best in the major leagues, but the following year he had a bad season. Everything seemed to go from bad to worse, and eventually he disappeared from the game. One year of success was no guarantee of future successes. For whatever reason, Larson's "ax"—his pitching arm—became dull, and he drifted off into obscurity.[62]

Too many people think that once an ax is sharp, it's always sharp. When this happens, they fall into complacency and become lazy or unfocused. The apostle James called this being double-minded.

> If any of you lacks wisdom, let him ask of God, who gives to all liberally and without reproach, and it will be given to him. But let him ask in faith, with no doubting, for he who doubts is like a wave of the sea driven and tossed by the wind. For let not that man suppose that he will receive anything from the Lord; he is a double-minded man, unstable in all his ways.
>
> James 1:5-8

Keep your "ax" sharp by continually seeking wisdom from the Lord and asking for whatever you need from Him without doubting He will provide what you ask. Your "ax" was specifically fashioned for you to enable you to do what He has called you to do. He isn't going to do it for you, but He is always there to help you. All you have to do is ask for His help.

2: Focus on success, not failure.

As you learn how to exercise your "ax," focusing on success is very important because focusing on failure is dangerous. Karl Wallenda, the famous tightrope walker, fell to his death in San Juan,

Puerto Rico in 1978. In an interview after the fall, his wife said, "All Karl thought about for three straight months was failing."[63] With his focus on failing, Karl Wallenda was destined to fall. Broken focus led to his death.

Many people are trying to tiptoe to the grave without ever having a failure. This isn't realistic. It is said that unsuccessful people fail approximately 3 out of 5 times. Conversely, successful people fail 2 out of 5 times. That's not a lot of difference.

A dartboard has a bull's-eye in the center worth 100 points. The remaining concentric rings are worth 80, 60, 40, and 20 points. If you don't aim for the bull's-eye, you'll probably hit zero every time. Someone once said, "I would rather attempt to do something great for God and fail, than to do nothing and succeed."[64]

Failure is not final! Abraham Lincoln once said, "My great concern is not whether you have failed, but whether you are content with your failure."[65]

Exercise your "ax" successfully by focusing on God's Word and His promises, then add your faith and be a doer. Remember God is with you and that guarantees your success.

Meditate on the words of this Scripture and poem:

Finally, brethren, whatever things are true, whatever things are noble, whatever things are just, whatever things are pure, whatever things are lovely, whatever things are of good report, if there is any virtue and if there is anything praiseworthy—meditate on these things.

Philippians 4:8

WHEN IT LOOKS LIKE I HAVE FAILED

Lord, are You trying to tell me something?

For...

Failure does not mean I'm a failure,

   It does mean I have not yet succeeded.

Failure does not mean I have accomplished nothing,

   It does mean I have learned something.

Failure does not mean I have been a fool,

   It does mean I have enough faith to experiment.

Failure does not mean I've been disgraced,

   It does mean I dared to try.

Failure does not mean I don't have it,

   It does mean I have to do something in a different way.

Failure does not mean I am inferior,

   It does mean I am not perfect.

Failure does not mean I've wasted my life,

   It does mean I have an excuse to start over.

Failure does not mean I should give up,

   It does mean I must try harder.

Failure does not mean I'll never make it,

   It does mean I need more patience.

Failure does not mean You have abandoned me,

It does mean You must have a better idea.[66]

TAKE ACTION TODAY

1) What do you do, or what would you like to do, that brings you joy and excitement? (Write out a list.)

2) What gifts and talents do you need to do these things?

3) How does your list line up with the God-given dreams, vision, or goals you identified earlier? (Cross off anything on the list that doesn't line up with His purpose.)

4) What existing skills need to be sharpened or what new skills need to be developed to accomplish your purpose?

5) What steps will you take in the next 30 days to prepare and develop your "ax"?

6) What will you do to keep your "ax" sharp?

Chapter 8

Taste the Results of Total Focus

"Never give up, for that is just the place
and time that the tide will turn."[67]

Harriet Beecher Stowe

Regardless of where you are right now—at the top of the mountain of success or at the bottom of the deepest valley of despair—your best is yet to come. This is not just a trite statement. God wants you to have His very best. That means there is always more to come, another mountain to climb, another level to reach, because God's call is an upward call. He doesn't want you to stay in your last success or your last failure. He wants you to let go of what is behind you and take ownership of what is ahead. He wants you to taste the results of total focus.

Too many Christians accept life as it comes to them and assume it is God's will. Such people experience unhappiness, not because they aren't born again and going to heaven or because God doesn't have the answer to every situation. It's because they make the wrong assumptions about God and put a question mark where God put a period!

Such assumptions spoke volumes to the person who said, "Unhappiness is not knowing what we want and killing ourselves to get it." Unhappy people don't know what they want, much less what they really can have. Because of that, they don't know what to focus on. They try so desperately to make something out of life that they wear themselves out and never attain happiness or satisfaction.

JUMP A LITTLE HIGHER

Everyone goes through battles, stresses, and frustrations in life, but the best word in that statement is "through." No one has to stay there unless he allows his mind to hold him captive by accepting the condition or situation as permanent. This reminds me of a story about a man who took a shortcut through a graveyard one night and fell into a freshly dug grave. Try as he might, he couldn't find a way out. He scratched and clawed and screamed but couldn't climb out. He finally accepted the fact he would have to wait until morning for someone to come help him get out of the grave.

Another man walking along the road tried taking the same shortcut through the graveyard and fell into the same hole. He struggled and struggled to climb out with no success and said, "I don't know if I can get out of this place."

Just as the second man was about to give up, a voice came from the corner behind him, "It's no use. You can't get out." Instantaneously, the second man found his way out of that grave.

What happened? When the second man was about to accept what had happened to him, he suddenly had a new level of motivation, and said, "Whoa, I'm out of here." He found out he could jump higher than he thought he could.

God is saying to you, "You don't have to stay where you are. I have a better plan. Focus on Me and jump a little higher. Come see what I have for you."

TWO REASONS PROGRESS DOESN'T HAPPEN

There are two reasons people don't move on from where they are:

1) They won't let go of what is holding them back, or

2) They never press in to what lies ahead because they fear the future.

Such a person stops living at a very early age. His tombstone reads: "Died at 21. Buried at 65." That means he gave up on his dreams and stopped trying to move forward. Even though he was still breathing, he stopped living at an early age. He just drifted along and existed for years without any purpose or meaning to his life until he died. What a tragedy.

If you find yourself circling the wagons and going nowhere but in circles, be assured God has made a way of escape. He has made a pathway out of every situation. God established that fact before the foundation of the earth. In other words, there isn't a thing the devil can do that faith can't fix. You simply have to "focus" your faith on different results.

FOCUS IS A CHOICE

Each person has a choice to be either a *wandering generality*—a jack-of-all-trades but a master of none—or to be a *meaningful specific*—someone who is focused on a goal. Being focused is the difference between good and best. Let's see what the apostle Paul says about focusing on the goal. Pay particular attention to the highlighted portions as you read an excerpt from *The Message Bible*.

> I'm not saying that I have this all together, that I have it made. But I am well on my way, reaching out for Christ, who has so wondrously reached out for me. Friends, don't get me wrong: By no means do I count myself an expert in all of this, but **I've got my eye on the goal,** where God is beckoning us onward—to Jesus. I'm off and running, and I'm not turning back.
>
> **So let's keep focused on that goal,** those of us who want everything God has for us. If any of you have something else in mind, something less than total commitment, God will clear your blurred vision—you'll see it yet! Now that we're on the right track, let's stay on it. Stick with me, friends, Keep track of those you see running this same course, headed for this same goal. There are many out there taking other paths, choosing other goals, and trying to get you to go along with them. I've warned you of them many times; sadly, I'm having to do it again. All they want is easy street. They hate Christ's Cross. But easy street is a dead-end street.
>
> Philippians 3:12-19 MESSAGE

Paul had focus, and we know he was a man of faith because he was looking ahead at something he did not yet have.

Paul got to where he was because he focused on the goal in faith. He didn't just wander around without any plan or purpose. His eye was focused.

If you choose to be a *meaningful specific*, you must make a decision that you are going to be a person of focus. Then you must determine on what you will focus, because whatever you focus upon will grow and multiply. That to which you give your attention will increase and become better. There are many wonderful goals we can strive for but only a few are worthy of our time and attention. Doing too many things always keeps us from doing our best, because the person who begins *too much* accomplishes *too little*.

FIVE STEPS TO GOD'S BEST

God wants our vision to be clearly focused so we can obtain everything He has for us. In the verses we just read from Philippians 3, Paul outlined five steps to laying hold of all God wants us to have. These steps spell out an acrostic for the word "focus."

1) Focus on the Goal

2) Overcome Indifference

3) Conquer Worry, Fear, Panic, and Paralysis

4) Undo "Blurred Vision"

5) Stop Hanging with Unfocused Friends

Step 1: Focus on the Goal—Jesus (the Word)

Jesus *is* the Word of God, and it is the Word that gives us life and power. If you focus on the Word, nothing can stop you from obtaining God's promise.

> In the beginning was the Word, and the Word was with
> God, and the Word was God.
>
> John 1:1

> For the word of God is living and powerful, and sharper
> than any two-edged sword, piercing even to the division of
> soul and spirit, and of joints and marrow, and is a discerner
> of the thoughts and intents of the heart.
>
> Hebrews 4:12

BLESSINGS IN THE DESERT

Did you know God brings forth rivers of blessings in the desert? Sometimes that is a hard truth to swallow, but God puts us where we are to do something with what we've got. Sometimes where He puts us is not where we want to be, and we don't like what we have to do while we are there. We don't want to be in the desert eating manna. We want to be at our favorite restaurant eating steak and lobster. However, if we just stay focused on Jesus and use what He has given us with the right attitude, He rewards our faithfulness in ways that surprise us every time.

After graduating from college, I was ready to step into the architectural field big time. I had my USC diploma and I was going places. God opened an incredible door for me at a nationally acclaimed architectural firm in Santa Monica, California. I was ready to design award-winning houses and buildings and show the world what I could do. Hey, I was a USC grad and that meant something!

ON MY WAY TO THE TOP

My first assignment was a far cry from my lofty expectations. In fact, I felt like it was an insult to my intelligence. Believe me, I was even tempted to walk off the job that first day when instead of drawing pencils and tracing paper, I was handed a garden rake and told to go up on the roof and rake the leaves from around the oak trees growing there.

My conversation was not edifying as I raked those leaves, complaining with every stroke. "What am I doing up here? After five years of college and tens of thousands of scholarship dollars being spent on my education, they send me to the roof to rake leaves! I could have done that without a scholarship and without a diploma!"

I convinced myself this was just a one-time, incidental job as I went back down to the office and reported I had finished the task. I quickly discovered the fallacy of my assumption when the supervisor said, "Okay. Put the rake over there. Here's a broom. Go out on Santa Monica Boulevard and sweep the sidewalk."

Sweep? I said to myself, *Doesn't he know how many USC graduates might see me out there? I told everybody I was going to work for one of the most reputable and well-known architectural firms in the nation. What will they think if they see me sweeping the sidewalk?*

AN "EDUCATED" STREET SWEEPER

I took that broom and swept the sidewalk, and I just knew all the people in those cars going by were saying, "Look at that errand boy." I wanted to pull out my diploma and say, "I have a diploma to do this. I'm educated. Yeah, it takes an education to sweep these streets!" If anyone honked, I never turned around or looked toward the street. I had a serious problem with that situation.

At that time Kuna and I were attending a Bible study, and I was so disturbed that I shared with the group what was happening at my new job. I said, "I don't know why God put me there. I don't know why I'm on the roof and out sweeping the sidewalk and doing such menial things. I have a diploma."

I was young and not very spiritual at the time. Then one of the ladies at the Bible study said, "Well, maybe God is trying to humble you."

JUST DO YOUR BEST

As upset as I was with her statement, I knew in my spirit that God wasn't doing anything to try to hurt me. This routine of odd jobs continued for three weeks or more. Every day I went home and prayed, because I didn't know if I was supposed to be there. I was convinced this couldn't be God, but something on the inside of me said, "Do your best." I kept saying, "But I don't want to do my best. I want them to find somebody else to do this job." That voice inside kept saying, "Do your best wherever you are."

I complained to Kuna, the Bible study group, and anyone who would listen. Finally, God got my attention and I started using my faith. I changed my attitude and began to believe God for new opportunities. It wasn't easy because nothing I saw pointed toward any change in my assignments.

ACTIVATING FAITH

One of the designers was a USC graduate, and he taunted me saying, "Oh, it took me years to get where I'm at now." I swallowed hard every time he said that.

I know I sounded ridiculous to him when I said, "It's not going to take me years. I'm believing God that a door is going to open for me to be designing."

"There's no way you're going to do that," he would say.

Others around him confirmed what he was telling me and said, "We don't have room for you. You're the new kid on the block. It took him (referring to the other USC grad) years to get on the design table. Besides, to design you have to come up with some creative ideas."

I went home and had a conversation with God. I said, "Lord, You planted me there and I appreciate that. But, Father, I'm believing that You're going to open a door for me to get on that design table faster than anyone has ever seen it happen in that company."

BELIEVING, CONFESSING, AND FOCUSING

I believed and confessed it all the while I was raking and sweeping. I stopped complaining and started focusing my faith. After about four weeks, the supervisor came to me and said, "I don't understand this, but the boss says he wants you to start designing at that table over there. He wants you to start working on some residential designs."

I jumped right in and started designing. It was the beginning of a wonderful relationship with the boss, Mr. Jones. Kuna and I were invited to his home several times. We were even able to minister to him at the hospital when he was dying. God gave us great favor because I learned how to focus my faith instead of complaining or leaving the place where He had placed me.

God knows where you are, where you need to be, *and* how to get you there. If you follow God's way and focus your faith, He will get you to where He wants you to be.

Step 2: Overcome indifference.

In order to have all that God has for us, we must overcome indifference by refocusing on the goal and pressing on to where God wants us to be. Indifference is a dangerous state of mind. It is defined as "absence of compulsion to or toward one thing or another."[68] Other synonyms are apathy, lack of enthusiasm, detachment, lack of interest. Clearly, indifference is a dream killer.

BEWARE OF THE DREAM KILLER

People who are indifferent lack commitment and focus. They are easily distracted and drift from one thing to another without ever really accomplishing anything significant. They may have had a dream at one time, but because of their lack of focus, it died long ago. They let their "ax" get dull.

The writer of the book of Hebrews warns us of the danger of indifference.

> So we must listen very carefully to the truths we have heard or we may drift away from them...what makes us think that we can escape if we are indifferent to this great salvation announced by the Lord himself?
>
> Hebrews 2:1,3 TLB

King Solomon also warns believers not to be indifferent.

> If you are slack in the day of distress, your strength is limited.
>
> Proverbs 24:10 NAB

In contrast, the writer of Hebrews also shares the positive aspects of believers staying focused on where God is taking them.

> Knowing what lies ahead for you, you won't become bored with being a Christian, nor become spiritually dull and indifferent, but you will be anxious to follow the example of those who receive all that God has promised them because of their strong faith and patience.
>
> Hebrews 6:12 TLB

If you have fallen into the trap of indifference, I want you to know that the Spirit of God is ready to confirm the Word in your life to get you re-motivated. A lot of people attend secular motivational seminars thinking that is the answer to getting out of their stagnant indifference, but all they are is a "quick fix" for the moment. It takes the blood of Jesus to wash away the pain and hurts of the past, and it takes the Holy Spirit to rise up within you to cause you to be productive in areas that you could not be in your natural self. Only the nature of God can take you beyond your own ability. When you find your sufficiency and strength *in Christ,* all things are possible.

Pray and ask the Holy Spirit to breathe the living Word into you with revelation knowledge of the Scriptures to move you out of your complacency and indifference. Find key Scriptures to speak over yourself and your circumstances throughout the day, such as, "I can do all things through Christ who strengthens me" (Phil. 4:13). Remember, God only responds to His Word spoken through you in faith.

Step 3: Conquer worry, fear, panic, and paralysis that come when you face difficult circumstances.

The devil is the author of fear. He uses fear as a powerful weapon to cripple and destroy God's people. Did you know fear can actually cause physical illness and even death? Doctors have diagnosed something called a panic attack. In such cases, the stress of life, the worries and concerns, the things carried around in a person's heart and mind, reach a point where they actually cause the body to go into physical distress. The heart rate and body temperature go crazy, sometimes even causing a heart attack. The person's whole body begins to panic because of what is going on mentally and emotionally. People who suffer from panic attacks become so focused on their fear they cannot function. They are crippled by it.

The word *fear* appears in the Bible over 400 times, including over 175 "fear not" statements. God wouldn't tell us to "fear not," if there wasn't something to fear. Even though we have an enemy, there is no reason to fear. Jesus defeated Satan on the cross. The

Word clearly tells us not to focus on fear and gives us instructions how to overcome it.

JUST TRUST JESUS

In John 14, Jesus tells us not to let our hearts be troubled, because He was going to prepare a place for us and promised to come back for us. He reassures us that He is the way, the truth, and the life; He is the only way to the Father. He promises that if we believe in Him and in His works, we will do greater works than He and our prayers will be answered. He promises that we will not be left alone but will have the Holy Spirit as our Helper, Comforter, and Teacher. Finally, He tells us that He gives us the greatest antidote to fear—His peace, a greater peace than the world can ever know.

Jesus was telling us that He has taken care of our tomorrow and all we have to do is trust Him.

Fear is nothing more than fiery darts from the enemy sent to disrupt our lives and to try to stop us from fulfilling God's purpose. A friend who has a deliverance and inner healing ministry said that fear is the predominant stronghold operating in the lives of people who come for ministry.

THE OPPOSITE OF FEAR IS FAITH

The way to overcome fear is to activate faith. One of the pieces of battle armor God has given us is "the shield of faith with which you will be able to quench all the fiery darts of the wicked one" (Eph. 6:16).

Do you put your armor on each day? Once you put it on, are you "praying always with all prayer and supplication in the Spirit" (Eph. 6:18)? Putting on the armor is only one step in withstanding the enemy. It is prayer that makes it work.

When David went out to meet Goliath, he didn't see a giant. He saw an uncircumcised Philistine who had the audacity to defy the armies of the living God. (1 Sam. 17:26.) King Saul's armies had been quaking in their sandals for forty days afraid to challenge the enemy. Young David came along and took up the challenge. He didn't let fear enter the picture. He was confident he could defeat the enemy because he had previous experiences with impossible situations—killing a lion and a bear with his bear hands—that built his faith.

TAKE AN OFFENSIVE STAND

David was totally focused on his goal, not just killing the giant, but glorifying the Lord of Hosts. He took the offensive by speaking boldly in the name of the Lord and running toward the enemy with his shield of faith firmly in place. David knew the battle wasn't his but the Lord's. It wasn't the tiny little stone flung from David's slingshot that killed Goliath. It was David's faith that made it happen. He had overcome fear long before he faced Goliath. David had already tasted the results of total focus and knew God was with him, just as He is with you in every trial and difficult circumstance.

On a daily basis, put on the armor God has given you, take an offensive stand, and run forward using your shield of faith to quench every fiery dart that the enemy shoots toward you. Then defeat him with your sword, which is the Word of God!

When you activate your faith and move offensively against the enemy, you will be able to count it all joy when temptations and trials come toward you. As your faith is tested, you learn patience and endurance, which results in a higher level of spiritual maturity or completeness in Christ.

> Consider it a sheer gift, friends, when tests and challenges come at you from all sides. You know that under pressure, your faith-life is forced into the open and shows its true colors. So don't try to get out of anything prematurely. Let it do its work so you become mature and well-developed, not deficient in any way.
>
> James 1:2-4 MESSAGE

> Do not sorrow, for the joy of the Lord is your strength.
>
> Nehemiah 8:10

Fear does not come from God. Stand up to fear with the Word of God, and the enemy will back down every time. Keep this verse in your arsenal of warfare Scriptures and speak it out loud when fear comes at you.

> For God has not given us a spirit of fear, but of power and of love and of a sound mind.
>
> 2 Timothy 1:7

Step 4: Undo "blurred vision," double-mindedness, or multiple vision.

Have you ever been to the eye doctor and had drops put in your eyes to dilate the pupils? It causes a strange sensation when you look at the eye chart and everything is blurry. Let's say your eye doctor has his office in the mall; and after your eye examination, you decide to do some shopping while the effects of the eye drops wear off. As you look through the merchandise at the store, you can't read the price tags. Then you decide to call home to let your family know it will be a while before you can drive, but when you take out your cell phone, you have a hard time focusing on the buttons to dial the number. It is frustrating not to be able to make your eyes come into focus. Even your glasses won't help. You're totally ineffective in performing routine tasks.

That is the way it is when you are trying to look at your future without focusing on any particular goal or purpose. When you have blurred vision, you can look through the sight of a rifle; but instead of one target, you see multiple targets, and you don't know at which one to aim your shot. If you are unsure of the future you have in Christ, you have blurred vision.

Many people have an unclear picture of what a life in Christ is going to do for them. They think that if they hook up with God, if they get saved and go the Jesus route, they won't be able to fulfill their dreams or do what they want to do in life. Unfortunately, they have a distorted view of what they think they have to give up rather than what they are going to gain. So, they struggle while trying to do things their way and never find peace or fulfillment in anything they do.

STEP INTO UNCHARTED WATERS

The only way to undo blurred vision is to focus on Jesus and His Word. I want you to be confident today that you can step into tomorrow with Jesus and live well. In these days in which we live, God is going to call you to step into a territory I call "uncharted waters," where you may have never before traveled. Nevertheless, if you allow yourself to be led by the Spirit and step out in faith, regardless of what you are leaving behind, God will give you more than you can imagine. He doesn't make mistakes; His timing is perfect, and He doesn't quit on His children. Even when we make mistakes, He doesn't give up on us.

BUILD YOUR FOUNDATION ON THE WORD

If you are going to move forward from where you are, you're going to have to make decisions based on God's Word. When you start building the foundation of your life and your decisions on the Word, you begin to move forward. God draws you further into your destiny through His promises, because the only thing He is bound to is His Word. His Word is a covenant, or a contract, with us. That is why we can't do anything or be successful without the promises of God.

The devil will do everything in his power to keep you ignorant of God's promises, because a believer with the Word of God in his mouth is deadly to the kingdom of darkness. You are a threat to every plan the devil devises against the human race. You can annihilate his plans with the Word. You can't do it in your physical strength. Only by being led by the Holy Spirit and by speaking the Word can you destroy the devil's plots in the spiritual realm.

MAKE THE WORD YOUR STANDARD

Focus on getting the Word of God into your mind, your soul, and your spirit until it is the measure, or standard, for everything you do. Spend time in the Word on a daily basis. There are many tools available in Christian bookstores to teach you how to study the Bible.

Develop an arsenal of Scriptures that apply to specific circumstances you may face. There are many topical Bibles in bookstores that will help you categorize specific Scriptures for different aspects of daily living. Do whatever it takes to get focused on the goal—Jesus and His Word—and undo your blurred vision.

Step 5: Stop hanging with unfocused friends.

To taste the results of total focus you must disassociate yourself from people who are unfocused or who aren't running the same race you are running. In a previous chapter, we explored in depth the importance of eliminating limiting relationships. I want to again emphasize how important it is to choose your friends and relationships wisely.

In the beginning of this chapter, we read the passage from Philippians 3 in which Paul emphasized the fact that there are many people following different paths who will try to draw you away from your goal, purpose, and destiny. He said, "All they want is an easy street. They hate Christ's cross. But an easy street is a dead-end street."

We all know people who don't think they need God. They may appear to be living on easy street and moving forward without Him because it's easy to be ungodly in this world. Just be careful that you don't start envying their ungodly ways. They may be getting somewhere for a season, but they will never reach their full potential or find true happiness without God. Eventually they will find themselves in a dead-end street, and you don't want to be in the car with them when they do.

TAKE THE HIGH ROAD

God has more for you than a dead-end street. He has called you to take the high road, to live and dwell with Him in heavenly places. You won't be on that high road alone. God has called others to walk with you, fitly joined together to make up the body of Christ. Each one has been given a gift to help fulfill a specific purpose for His kingdom. Together, you will do what He has called you to do, be what He has created you to be, and taste the results of total focus.

TAKE ACTION TODAY

1) What track marks are you leaving behind you that indicate you are focused on the things God has for you?

2) What changes do you need to make to be focused on Christ rather than on what you think you can do in your own ability?

3) When something goes wrong, what is the first thing you measure it against?

4) What do you plan to do to become more Word-oriented?

Chapter 9

{ Let the Reproofs of Instruction Be Your Way of Life }

"We cannot become what we need to
be by remaining what we are."[69]

John C. Maxwell

What was your response the last time someone pointed out an area in your life that needs to be improved or changed? Perhaps it was your last performance review at work, or maybe it was when your spouse or a family member expressed a concern about the manner in which you treated him or her.

Think about this question carefully before you answer and be totally honest with yourself. Did you immediately become angry and defensive or start looking at the other person's faults? Or, did you ponder what this person was saying and consider what you could do to move to a higher level of performance or communication?

The way you responded is a clear indication of whether or not you allow the reproofs of instruction to be your way of life. In other words, it is a measure of how spiritually mature you really are and whether you are moving forward and reaching upward.

This strategy of letting the reproofs of instruction be our way of life may be one of the most difficult for many of us to apply to our lives in this country that thrives on independence and rebels against authority on every level. That is why God's Word must be our guide in seeking a better way of life, because it lights the path to success. We must seek illumination and understanding from the Word and be balanced in the Word. A little dab won't do!

> For the commandment is a lamp, and the law a light;
> Reproofs of instruction are the way of life.
>
> Proverbs 6:23

The words, commandment, law, and Word of God are all interchangeable. In this Scripture and numerous others, we learn that the Word lights the path for us to live a godly life as it directs our steps. Psalm 119 is a lengthy passage, but it is filled with insight into how the Word of God, His commandments, provides instruction, illumination, and teaching for a successful way of life.

> Your word is a lamp to my feet and a light to my path.
>
> Psalm 119:105

We should welcome His reproofs and instructions because they are meant for our good. The word *reproof,* or *reprove,* comes from the root word *rebuke.*[70] The difference is that *reprove* suggests scolding or correcting gently or with kindly intent, whereas *rebuke* suggests a sharp or stern correction. Wouldn't you rather receive a loving reproof than ignore instruction and receive a rebuke?

When I reprove one of my daughters, I'm not trying to jump on her case. I don't enjoy having to confront her. She may not understand it right then, but I am trying to show her a better way of doing things. When it comes to training my daughters, I have to speak godly principles from the Word of God into their lives and challenge them to grow and mature in all areas of life—physically, emotionally, and spiritually. When I correct them, I am proving that I love them just as our heavenly Father shows His love to us through correction.

> My son, do not despise the chastening of the Lord; nor detest His correction. For whom the Lord loves He corrects, just as a father the son (*or daughter*) in whom he delights.
>
> Proverbs 3:11,12

Making godly changes initiates progress on the right pathway of life. It is a fool who doesn't hear God but expresses his own heart and will. Correction, instruction, and training show a better way, because change is *the* way of life, not *a* way of life. Positive change produces progress, one step at a time, moving upward continuously.

MOVEMENT DOESN'T GUARANTEE PROGRESS

It is important to note that movement doesn't necessarily mean change is taking place or that progress is being made. A wheel may be spinning in a rut and a rocking chair may be rocking, but neither one is moving forward.

A man complained to his boss that he didn't receive a promotion he felt he deserved. "After all, he argued, I've had twenty-five years of experience."

His boss replied, "No, Joe, that's where you're wrong. You have had one year's experience twenty-five times."[71]

Doing something repeatedly does not mean learning or growth has taken place. It's not making the same mistake over and over that produces change. It's what we do with what we have learned from the mistake that produces different results. Someone once said, "If you keep doing what you've been doing, you're going to keep getting what you've been getting." Change involves moving from one level to another level. I particularly like the wisdom expressed by Clayton G. Orcutt when he said, "Change itself is not progress, but change is the price that we pay for progress."[72]

RIGHTEOUS REPROOFS ARE A KINDNESS

David was a man after God's own heart, and he wanted to be told of his faults by his friends and family. He saw it as a kindness to bring him into repentance for his sins and to prevent relapses into sin.

> Let the righteous strike me; it shall be a kindness. And let him rebuke me; it shall be as excellent oil; let my head not refuse it. For still my prayer is against the deeds of the wicked.
>
> Psalm 141:5

From David's example, we learn how to take specific steps to receive righteous reproofs:

- Choose or have the desire to be told of our faults or weaknesses.

- Accept it as a kindness to bring about good in our lives.

- Bear it patiently.

- Determine to be helped and healed by it.

- Pray for our enemies continuously even as they do evil.

Being reproved doesn't feel good. It cuts to the quick and makes us face reality. It is humbling and at times painful. It forces us to change in two areas: internally and externally.

Internally, I have to deal with changing my thoughts, attitudes, behavior, and character. If I don't do this, I will end up playing a game of denial saying, "There's nothing wrong with me. It's everyone else's fault. I'm the victim and everyone is against me!"

Externally, I have to deal with the change going on around me. People change. Circumstances and events change. Times change and society changes. Nothing stays the same or stands still.

CHANGE IS INEVITABLE

The one constant that we can count on is that change is inevitable. Just when we get into a groove that feels good and seems to be working something shifts and changes. Think about this on a corporate level. If a company doesn't change with the times, what happens to that company? It begins to die. In today's global market, many companies have been forced out of business or have been gobbled up by larger, more aggressive conglomerates. It doesn't matter how good the company was ten years ago. If it doesn't stay on top of today's market, it isn't going to be profitable.

Technology is changing our world moment by moment. It is almost impossible to keep up with the changes. Buy a top-of-the-line computer today, and another model comes along tomorrow with more speed and features to make yours obsolete. Have you experienced the frustration of learning how to use email and cell phones only to have new technology make you feel ignorant all over again? Worse yet, have you ever had to ask your child to help you figure it out?

Change isn't easy. It can be uncomfortable, frustrating, challenging, and nerve wrenching, but we can't stop it. If we choose to stand still, the world and everyone around us will simply pass us by. If we're going to have vibrant, growing relationships, then we have to be continually learning, growing, and maturing.

Kuna and I have been married for over 19 years, and we knew each other for five years before we married. The way in which we react to one another, how our personality types mesh or clash, and the way we communicate with each other have changed immensely over the years. Our relationship has grown and is still changing. It has been a challenge for both of us. There hasn't been any shedding of blood but there has been a lot of sweat and tears. If we hadn't learned that change is "the" way of life, we might not have made it.

Let's explore five hindrances to change.

1. Pride: "I don't need to change."

We have all seen Mr. or Ms. Pride at work in relationships saying, "I don't have a problem. Something is wrong with you. I'm just fine." Another common statement is, "I know I'm not perfect, but you're the one who needs to change in this relationship."

Beware of pride. It is a stumbling block that is guaranteed to trip you up. Here's what the Word says.

Pride goes before destruction, and a haughty spirit before a fall.

Proverbs 16:18

Don't let pride keep you from being all God has called you to be.

2. Fear: "I'm afraid to take the risk."

Some people fear change to the extent they will hang on to something mediocre rather than risk stepping into something new. How many women have married men they knew were not right for them because they didn't think they would get another chance at marriage?

Too many times people hang on to their beliefs and attitudes because it is all they know. It's their security blanket.

The truth is, you cannot have what God has for you unless you give up what you have. If your hand isn't empty, He can't fill it with His best.

It is time to get rid of fear and step out of your boat. Keep your eyes on Jesus and you won't sink.

Love has been perfected among us in this: that we may have boldness in the day of judgment; because as He is, so are we in this world. There is no fear in love; but perfect love casts out fear, because fear involves torment. But he who fears has not been made perfect in love.

1 John 4:17,18

Learn to love as Jesus loved and you won't have to struggle with the crippling effects of fear every time change knocks on your door.

3. Rebellion: "I don't want to change."

This is a battle of the will and the flesh. I've heard church people say, "That sounds good, Preacher, but I don't want to do that." Or, "I think people should get involved, but I don't do that sort of thing."

This is no different from a little child who stamps his foot and says, "I don't want to do that," or who puts his hands over his ears and screams, "I'm not listening to you!"

When we refuse to do what God has told us to do, it is pure rebellion. Who are we to tell the Father what is best for us? Rebellion is a dangerous ground on which to be walking. King Saul lost his kingdom because of it.

> Behold, to obey is better than sacrifice, and to heed than the fat of rams. For rebellion is the sin of witchcraft and stubbornness is as iniquity and idolatry. Because you have rejected the word of the Lord, He also has rejected you from being king.
>
> 1 Samuel 15:22,23

Don't lose the destiny God has for you by letting rebellion rule in your life.

4. Laziness: "I don't feel like it."

Some feel it is too hard or too much work to change. It has become socially acceptable not to change and to accept where we are right now in our lives. When we do this, we end up living a mediocre life right along with everyone else; and it appears as though we're doing just fine.

We have become a society of "couch potatoes." We'd rather stay home and watch a TV sitcom than to come back to church on Sunday night. Let's see how that prospers your life.

What wisdom will you be able to pull from that TV show when you have to make a decision about a business deal that will either make or break your business? Or, what advice will you learn from any of the sitcoms that will enable you to ace your job interview?

Poverty comes through laziness. If you are too lazy to study the Bible and show yourself approved, don't expect to see your life prospering.

> How long will you lie there, you sluggard? When will you get up from your sleep? A little sleep, a little slumber, a little folding of the hands to rest—and poverty will come on you like a bandit and scarcity like an armed man.
>
> Proverbs 6:9-11 NIV

5. Ignorance: "I've never thought about changing."

Some people don't know what God has for them or what their potential is. Ignorance is not an acceptable excuse to God. He has given us His Word, and it is up to us to search it and learn from it.

My people are destroyed for lack of knowledge.

Hosea 4:6

It is time to take charge of your life by asking the Holy Spirit what and how you need to change. Learn how to hear the Holy Spirit by spending time with Him in prayer, by staying plugged into the Word of God, and by staying focused on Him.

UNDER CONSTRUCTION

Accept the fact that you are continuously "under construction." Embrace change with a desire and willingness to grow and progress, because where you are isn't limited to what you are and current circumstances aren't your final resting place. Negative circumstances are always subject to change, but God and His Word never change.

Sometimes all it takes to grow or move up is a small change in your daily habits, a little different way of looking at things, or a willingness to get up one more time when you've been knocked down. Habits are deeply imbedded daily actions that can be either good or bad. Unchecked, they can result in a destiny not reached.

Your destiny is not to live where you are with the habits that hold you there. Your destiny is to continue to move and live at a higher level. John Maxwell said, "Every person who has become successful, has simply formed the habit of doing things that failures dislike doing and will not do."[73]

HABITS EXPRESS CHARACTER

Habits are powerful factors in our lives. Because they are consistent, often unconscious patterns, they constantly express our character and produce our effectiveness or ineffectiveness. Actually, our character is a composite of our habits. Consider the words of this poem carefully:

"Sow a thought, reap an action.

Sow an action, reap a habit.

Sow a habit, reap a character.

Sow a character, reap a destiny!"[74]

Habits can be learned *and* unlearned. A habit is not formed by doing something once or twice, except perhaps in the case of highly addictive drugs and sometimes with drinking alcohol. Normally, it requires repetitive action. Educator Horace Mann said, "Habits are like a cable. We weave a strand of it every day…."[75] The more strands of cable that are woven together, the more difficult it is to break it. I have heard it said that it takes 21 days to form a habit.

HABITS HAVE GRAVITY PULL

Habits are harder to change and more deeply imbedded in our lives than most people really want to admit. Those of us who watched the lunar voyage of Apollo 11 were transfixed as we saw the first men walk on the moon and return to earth. Superlatives such as "fantastic" and "incredible" were inadequate to describe those eventful days. But to get there, those astronauts literally had to break out of the tremendous *gravity pull* of the earth.

More energy was spent in the first few minutes of lift-off, in the first few miles of travel, than was used over the next several days to travel half a million miles. Habits, too, have tremendous *gravity pull.*

Breaking deeply imbedded habitual tendencies such as procrastination, impatience, criticalness, anger, selfishness, and indifference involve more than a little will power and major changes in our lives. "Lift-off" takes tremendous effort, but once we break out of "gravity's pull," freedom is the result.

Like any natural force, gravity's pull can work with us or against us. The gravity pull of some of our habits may be keeping us from going where we want to go. The good news is that we don't have to allow this to continue if we understand that changing a habit involves a process, time, and total commitment.

KEY INGREDIENTS OF A HABIT

Three ingredients must be present to change a habit:

1) Knowledge: the "what to do and why."

2) Skill: the "how to."

3) Desire: the "want to."

The knowledge required involves having an understanding of "new creation realities," who you are in Christ and what you can do in Christ. It means putting off the "old man" who lives according to old worldly habits and deeds and putting on the "new man" with new habits and new deeds according to the Spirit and Word of God. To do this you must renew your mind by drinking from the Living Water of the Word of God. Every believer who has asked Jesus to dwell in his or her heart can live as a new man or woman in Christ by gaining this knowledge of Him.

KNOWLEDGE + ACTION = RESULTS

Keep in mind that knowledge alone isn't enough. You can read the Bible all day long and learn new truths, but it won't do you a bit of good unless you put those truths into action. Knowledge not acted upon does not produce results.

The story of Gideon related in Judges 6 is a classic example of how important it is to act upon the knowledge the Lord gives us. Gideon was much like believers today, living with a "winepress mentality" instead of living a victorious life. Let me lay some groundwork of what was taking place here.

Israel had been living under the harsh, oppressive rule of the Midianites for seven years. Because of the impoverished social, economic, and incredibly demonic conditions forced upon them, the Israelite's attitudes reflected extremely low self-worth and fear. It wasn't God's desire for them to live this way, but they had stepped out from under His covering and protection by disobeying His commandments and getting involved in idolatry and other sins. This is much the way we live before we accept Jesus into our hearts.

Things were not going well for the people of Israel, and no matter what they tried to do to prosper or succeed, nothing seemed to work for them. Life became so hard that they finally cried out to God and repented for their rebellion and stubbornness.

God sent a prophet to speak to them and tell them that what they were going through wasn't His doing; but because they had cried out to Him, things were going to be different.

This is similar to what happens when we are "born again." We are living in sin, and when we get desperate enough to call out to God, He sends the Holy Spirit to us to tell us it wasn't His desire for us to live defeated lives and now things will be different.

Spiritually speaking, when a person is born on this earth, it is only a temporary home. Each person will live eternally either in heaven or hell. When a person chooses to ask Jesus to live in his heart, he is "born again" in the spiritual sense and secures his eternal home with God in heaven. Once this happens, unless he renews his mind—changes the way he thinks—with God's Word and then changes his daily habits, he will continue to live in the oppressive, defeated conditions in which he was living before accepting Christ.

Gideon and the people of Israel had heard the words of the prophet sent by God, but they had not renewed their minds and changed their habits. In this story we find Gideon, who had been liberated and set free by the words of the prophet, going back to the habit of living in the constraints and limitations of the wine press bound by fear. Many people in the body of Christ today know God's will, yet they go back to their habit of living in fear, doubt, and unbelief. It's like being in prison. The guard comes and unlocks the door and swings it wide open, but the prisoner stays in the cell because he thinks it is safer there.

ARE YOU LIVING A POSTAGE-STAMP LIFESTYLE?

Do you remember the story of the goldfish the little boy put in the lake at the end of the dock? Hours later the little fish was still swimming in circles as though it were still in its bowl. Many of us are living postage-stamp lifestyles on three-by-five cards because our minds are still bound by old habits. Jesus is shaking His head saying, "I set you free. Now live according to the new man." He has given us unlimited access to His Word. It is up to us to act on it.

> Put on the new man who is renewed in knowledge
> according to the image of Him who created Him.
>
> Colossians 3:10

LEARNING IS NOT CHANGING

Knowledge alone is not enough. John Maxwell explained this so well when he said, "I teach what I know, but I reproduce what I am."[76] It is amazing how much knowledge we actually have and yet we don't reproduce that knowledge in a practical sense to move us to a new level. The reason this happens is because learning is just learning, not changing.

You can learn a lot and change very little unless you have the desire and are willing to break the cycle of insanity and the comfort of compromise that really is producing the level at which you are living right now. Insanity is doing the same thing over and over again and expecting different results. It isn't going to happen. Compromise is accepting what you don't believe in because you refuse to fight for what you do believe in.

{ 183 }

If you are tired and fed up with where you are living or with anything in your life, you must be willing to change the habits that have produced these conditions in your life. Everything you do in life is done by habit.

How often do you drive to work on auto pilot? You don't even remember how you got there because your mind was running through the presentation you had to make to your boss or you were thinking about the fight you had with your spouse before you slammed the door and walked out. You have driven that route so many times it is imbedded in your subconscious. If you don't root out the habits you have imbedded in your mind, nothing is going to change in your life.

SKILLS ARE NECESSARY, TOO

Once you have the knowledge and the desire to change a habit, you must also have the necessary skills to do it. I have the desire to be a good communicator, and I've studied the Scriptures and many excellent books on communication to gather a considerable amount of knowledge on the subject. However, I have found I need to polish my listening skills. I am ineffective in my communication with staff or family members because I tend to tell them what I think without listening to what they have to say on the subject. My girls will say to me, "Dad, would you just listen to us?" I have to work on developing better listening skills and break my habit of talking too much and too soon. If I don't apply these skills, all my knowledge and desire are wasted.

FORM HABITS THAT PRODUCE RESULTS

Your greatest challenges are the habits that "make up" your current lifestyle. Consider these important keys when forming new habits that will produce new results:

1: *Evaluate the values you say you value.*

There are a lot of things we say we value but haven't incorporated them into our lives by forming daily habits around them. We need to put each thing we value to a test. For example, you may say you value studying the Word of God. Test your true value with this question, "How much time do I spend studying the Word each day?" Your answer will speak for itself.

> Examine yourselves as to whether you are in the faith. Test yourselves. Do you not know yourselves, that Jesus Christ is in you?—unless indeed you are disqualified.
>
> 2 Corinthians 13:5

2: *Begin to see beyond where you are right now!*

Don't allow yourself to be so consumed with the problems and circumstances in your present that you forget to focus on the answer—the King of Kings and the Lord of Lords. Set your mind on things above, not on the things of this world. Get your eyes off what you are seeing in the natural and look at the spiritual aspects of the situation. Start praising and worshipping the Lord as an act of faith.

> Lift your eyes now and look from the place where you are.
>
> Genesis 13:14

3: *Don't accept the limitations of people around you. Remember who your God is!*

No one can hold you down unless you give him or her permission. Zig Ziglar has an acronym for this. He says, "Don't be a SNIOP!" A *SNIOP* is someone who is Susceptible to the Negative Influences of Other People.[77] If you are surrounded by a bunch of limited thinkers or limited talkers, start telling them about your *big* God. Put hope back in your life by giving God the praise He deserves to pull you out of whatever battle you are in today.

> But I will hope continually, and will praise You yet more and more. My mouth shall tell of Your righteousness and Your salvation all the day, for I do not know their limits. I will go in the strength of the Lord God; I will make mention of Your righteousness, of Yours only.
>
> Psalm 71:14-16

4: *Don't accept your own limitations.*

You know yourself better than anyone else does. Guard your thoughts and speak positive words. Pray Scripture over yourself such as "I have strength for all things in Christ Who empowers me [I am ready for anything and equal to anything through Him Who infuses inner strength into me; I am self-sufficient in Christ's sufficiency]" (Phil. 4:13 AMP).

God gives people great ideas, and He never provides a vision without a plan. Remember, Eli Whitney was laughed at when he publicized his cotton gin. Edison had to install his electric light free of charge in an office building before anyone would even look at it. The first sewing machine was smashed to pieces by a Boston mob. People scoffed at the idea of railroads. People thought that traveling thirty miles an hour would stop the circulation of the blood. Morse had to plead before ten Congresses before they would even look at his telegraph. The lesson is: don't give up.

5. *Live by vision, not by history (past) or current events (present circumstances).*

Let me emphasize again how important it is to clearly define where you are today and where you are going in the future. If you haven't already done this, take the time right now to go back and follow the seven steps outlined in Chapter 1 to write out your vision and goals. Then start talking like a visionary so people will know that you believe what your God can do and will do in your life. Now begin forming habits that will support your vision and goals, and take this Scripture to heart, "And the Lord said, 'Write my answer on a billboard, large and clear, so that anyone can read it at a glance and rush to tell the others. But these things I plan won't happen right away. Slowly, steadily, surely, the time approaches when the vision will be fulfilled. If it seems slow, do not despair, for these things will surely come to pass. Just be patient! They will not be overdue a single day!'" (Hab. 2:2,3 TLB).

DON'T RESIST CHANGE

Those who resist change cannot walk with God and fulfill His plan for their lives. God is never stagnant and anyone who is will be left behind. We must grow and get out of our "ruts" if we want to stay in "the" way of life.

I want to quickly examine two attitudes that are evidence of someone who is stuck in a rut. The first is the "I already know what the problem is" attitude. We may be having marriage problems, financial difficulties, health challenges, or leadership conflicts. If we are convinced we know what is causing these problems, we reject whatever wisdom someone else tries to share that is different from our opinion. We may unintentionally reject it verbally, outwardly, and sometimes internally.

A person with an "I already know it" attitude acts like a child who tells a parent, "Don't tell me that, I already know that!" When a financial counselor gives advice to this person, he says, "That won't work." A marriage counselor may speak into a struggling marriage, and such a person responds saying, "We tried that already. It won't work." That "been there, done that" attitude puts up an immediate barrier to change.

The second attitude we must guard against is the "isolation" attitude. Solomon talks about the fool who will not hear but only wants to express what he already knows.

> A man who isolates himself seeks his own desire; he rages against all wise judgment. A fool has no delight in understanding, but in expressing his own heart.
>
> Proverbs 18:1,2

Isolation doesn't mean you avoid being around people. It means you surround yourself only with people who agree with you. It's that "I'm okay, you're okay" mentality. You feel justified in your opinion as long as you don't talk with anybody who disagrees with you. When you do this, you refuse to accept wise judgment, because you only want to "believe" what you want to believe.

Examine your heart and ask yourself, "Whom do I avoid talking with or being around?" Do you quickly take an offensive stand when a friend or family member speaks a little "truth in love" to you? Do you try to turn the tables and bring up that person's faults to cover your own? Do you pick an argument to hide your own behavior?

CHANGE IS FOR YOUR BENEFIT

Don't let yourself get stuck in a "rut." Be prepared to move when God tells you to move and do what He tells you to do. Change is for your benefit, not to hold you back. The people of Israel learned this lesson while God was leading them through the wilderness to the Promised Land. You can read about it in Numbers 9:15-23.

They had built the tabernacle according to the Lord's instructions. During the day, a cloud covered the tabernacle; and at night, the cloud became a pillar of fire. The cloud provided shade from the sun during the day, and the fire provided warmth in the cold desert nights. When the cloud rose above the tabernacle and moved forward, the entire camp followed it. Wherever the cloud stopped was where they camped until the cloud moved again. When God said go, they went. They only moved when God moved. Without the cloud to provide direction, they didn't know where to go.

Suppose one night some of the Israelite families decided they were going to go watch the chariot races over in the next valley instead of going to the services at the tabernacle. While they were gone, the cloud moved. Imagine how surprised they

would have been when they came back to camp to find that everyone had gone ahead without them! To make matters worse, the
wind had kicked up and erased the tracks of the people from the
camp so there was no way to tell which direction to go to find the
rest of their people. Without the cloud, these families found themselves with no warmth at night, no shade in the day, no more
manna to eat, no more miracles, and no clear direction of where to
go. They were in a mess.

STAY WITH THE CLOUD

This story illustrates how important it is to stay with the
cloud, with God. Because without the cloud, there is no protection, and without the pillar of fire, there is no provision. We must
be ready to move when God says move. We must stay on the
cutting edge and open to the promptings of the Holy Spirit. We
must stay in fellowship with Him in His presence so we will know
where and when He wants us to go and what He wants us to do.

When we get out from under His protection, we start
crying, "Lord, why are You letting this happen to me?"

The Lord says, "It's not Me. I'm over here! By the way, why
are you over there?"

God is saying to us, "My miracles are still happening. The
pillar of fire is still hot. Come on over!"

Then He says, "When you get here, I want you to change
some things in your character. You need to forgive some people
from your past, and some of your bad attitudes have got to go. It

is your choice to stay where you are, but 'I AM' is going to keep moving on without you."

Does any of that conversation ring a bell in your spirit? We've all been there at some time or other. We have a choice of whether to follow the cloud or go our own way.

God is instructing us. We aren't here to instruct Him. He's the Potter, and we are the clay. He shapes our lives. He doesn't appreciate it when we try to shape Him into our image or liking. The children of Israel found themselves in all kinds of trouble when they rebelled against His authority and tried doing things their way. As long as we are being reproved and instructed, we are in "the" way of life, progressing and obtaining His approval, gaining understanding and wisdom as these Scriptures confirm:

> Listen to my counsel—oh, don't refuse it—and be wise.
> Happy is the man who is so anxious to be with me that he
> watches for me daily at my gates, or waits for me outside
> my home! For whoever finds me finds life and wins approval
> from the Lord. But the one who misses me has injured
> himself irreparably. Those who refuse me show that they
> love death.
>
> Proverbs 8:33-36 TLB

> Teach a wise man, and he will be the wiser; teach a good
> man, and he will learn more. For the reverence and fear of
> God are basic to all wisdom. Knowing God results in every
> other kind of understanding.
>
> Proverbs 9:9,10 TLB

TAKE ACTION TODAY

1) What was the latest specific change you made in your life that brought improvement?

2) What habits have your formed or will you form that others dislike or won't do?

3) What did you identify as your number one hindrance to change?

4) What action will you take to overcome this hindrance?

Chapter 10

{ Execute Your Power as a Fighter }

"No one can defeat us unless we first defeat ourselves.
Every one of us must be guided by this truth."[78]

Dwight D. Eisenhower

All of God's promises are available to anyone who believes and is willing to pay the price to obtain them. That price is a willingness to "fight"! Fighting may not sound very Christian, but when it comes to dealing with the enemy of your soul—the devil—God's Word does not endorse meekness or gentleness. It requires a fighting posture—a tough, ruthless, bulldog tenacity—because the devil hates you! You are a threat to his plans and purposes, and he will do whatever is necessary to take you out. Your willingness to fight is a matter of survival.

Winston Churchill was nicknamed "the bulldog" because he had a reputation for never quitting. He knew that quitters always lose the battle, and it was his determination that took England through its darkest days in World War II. The speech he gave on the day he became prime minister depicts the type of fighting spirit needed to defeat the enemy in the natural or the spiritual. Here is an excerpt of that speech.

"I have nothing to offer but blood, toil, tears, and sweat. You ask, 'What is our policy?' I will say: It is to wage war by sea, land, and air, with all our might and with all the strength God can give us. That is our policy. You ask, 'What is our aim?' I can answer in one word: It is victory. Victory at all costs. Victory in spite of all terror. Victory however long and hard the road may be; for without victory, there is no survival."[79]

DEVELOP A FIGHTING SPIRIT

You must accept the fact that the devil is your adversary and develop a fighting spirit to defeat him. That is why the apostle James said, "Submit yourselves, then, to God. Resist the devil, and he will flee from you" (James 4:7 NIV). If you don't resist him, he won't flee. He doesn't give up one inch of territory without a fight.

God is a God of war. He taught the Bible greats of the Old Testament how to fight, and that fighting spirit didn't stop in the New Testament. The Bible is a book of battles, and the Christian life is a fight of faith. As a new creation in Christ, you must learn to fight with the Word of God, the power of the Holy Ghost, and the blood of Jesus.

DON'T BE THE DEVIL'S DOORMAT

Tragically, a distorted theology has crept into the church and caused many believers to become a doormat for the devil. Such people passively accept whatever comes their way as "the will of God" for their lives. They attribute sickness and disease or poverty to God's will, thinking He is trying to teach them something by it.

They believe God initiates every tragedy or crisis for some greater or higher purpose that they will only understand in the "sweet by and by." Be careful to whom you are listening. The truth is God is not your enemy; the devil is. Get that settled in your spirit.

WHY DO YOU HAVE TO FIGHT?

The devil was defeated 2,000 years ago on a hill called Golgotha when Jesus Christ made the ultimate sacrifice for us by shedding His precious blood on the cross. You may be thinking, *Well,* if the devil was defeated, *why do I have to keep fighting him now?* The reason is that we must enforce his defeat.

When a battle is fought and won, the conquering army doesn't just walk away and say, "Whew, we sure are glad that's over. Now we can go home and get back to life the way it was before all this fighting." No, the conquering army must enforce the conditions of the victory to keep the enemy from coming back and infiltrating the perimeter that has been secured.

EXERCISE YOUR POWER OF ATTORNEY

Through His death and resurrection, Jesus defeated the devil, but He didn't destroy him, which means the devil is still present and real on the earth today. Jesus took back the authority Satan had stolen from Adam and Eve in the Garden of Eden and gave it to us. In other words, we have a "power of attorney" from Jesus to resist and fight the enemy on all fronts. We just have to exercise this authority according to God's principles.

FIGHT THE GOOD FIGHT OF FAITH

The apostle Paul was anything but passive. He never stopped pressing on toward the upward call of his life and toward the things God had for him. Paul was constantly in a battle, but he never quit. He gave young Timothy whom he was mentoring this advice:

> Fight the good fight of faith, lay hold on eternal life, whereunto thou art also called, and hast professed a good profession before many witnesses.
>
> 1 Timothy 6:12 KJV

In this verse Paul says, we have been called to "eternal life." The Greek word for "eternal life" is *zoe*, meaning "life as God has it."[80] That is life without sickness, disease, insufficiency, fear, strife, and anything else from the kingdom of darkness.

Many believers fail to understand that the blessings of "zoe life" don't fall out of heaven's supply and onto their head just because they are saved. I don't know why so many Christians misunderstand this. Yes, you are saved. You have the nature of God and are a new creation in Christ Jesus. The Greater One does live on the inside of you. However, all the blessings mentioned above don't come to you automatically even though you have a right to them. You have to lay hold of them by faith, and that means you have to fight for them.

If you have a treasure chest in your home but don't know where it is, you can't take it to the bank and cash in the treasure. It's the same way with the promises of God. You have to know where to find these promises in the Scriptures and learn how to use them in a practical, dynamic way. You have to be absolutely determined not to accept anything less than God's best for your life and fight the good fight of faith to lay hold of it. No one else can do it for you.

THE VIOLENT TAKE IT BY FORCE!

Passivity and resignation are at odds with the New Testament way of life. Jesus spoke of violence being waged against the kingdom of God when He said,

> And from the days of John the Baptist until the present time, the kingdom of heaven has endured violent assault, and violent men seize it by force [as a precious prize – a share in the heavenly kingdom is sought with most ardent zeal and intense exertion].
>
> Matthew 11:12 AMP

Jesus wasn't talking about heaven. He was talking about the kingdom of God here on the earth. He was talking about your being violent enough to lay hold of the promises of God, whether it's prosperity, healing, peace, His power, or joy. You are going to have to fight for these promises with ardent zeal and intensity. There is absolutely nothing that you as a believer cannot overcome if you have a fighting spirit and an unbreakable will to win.

THE BATTLE LINE IS DRAWN

Actually, you are already a winner, because the greatest battle was won when you crossed over the bloodline of Calvary and made a decision to accept Christ as your Savior. You belong to

Christ and nothing the enemy might try to do can take you out of God's hand. That was when the battle lines were drawn. The devil didn't care what you did until you made that decision. Now he is your adversary.

I want you to understand Satan. The devil is a real spiritual being. He is intensely interested in doing you harm. Don't take his ability to affect your life lightly. He is a very real and capable opponent.

> Be sober, be vigilant; because your adversary the devil walks about like a roaring lion, seeking whom he may devour.
>
> 1 Peter 5:8

Notice this verse says the devil is seeking whom he "may" devour. That means he is looking at you like a target, but it doesn't mean he can automatically take you down. You must do your part to guard your heart and rule over your spirit so you will be strong enough to resist whatever fiery darts the enemy throws at you.

RULE YOUR SPIRIT

Let me explain what I mean by ruling over your spirit. This is very important for you to understand. God created us as a three-part being. We have a spirit, a soul, and a body.

> Now may the God of peace Himself sanctify you completely; and may your whole spirit, soul, and body be preserved blameless at the coming of our Lord Jesus Christ.
>
> 1 Thessalonians 5:23

In God's order of things, our spirit is meant to rule over our soul, which in turn rules over our body or flesh. When we accept Jesus as Savior, our spirit is reborn. It is then up to us to learn how to keep our spirit strong by continually feeding it with the Word of God and praying. When our spirit is strong, we are able to lift up our shield of faith and ward off the fiery darts from the enemy. If we can't rule over our spirit, we will never be able to rule over our soul or our flesh. Let's look at some Scriptures on ruling our spirit.

> He who is slow to anger is better than the mighty, and he
> who rules his spirit than he who takes a city.
>
> Proverbs 16:32

Imagine how powerful an individual would be who could come in and take a fortified city. He would have armaments and strategies and many resources at his disposal. This really puts in perspective how powerful a person is who can rule his spirit.

THE BATTLEFIELD IS IN THE MIND

Our soul is made up of our mind, our will, and our emotions. The enemy's favorite battleground is in our mind, because he is the father of lies and deception. Did you know that 90 percent of the mistakes we make in life are in the emotional realm? Many of us have fallen down and scraped our spiritual knees when our emotions or mindset became stronger than our spirit. The only control you have over your soul and your flesh is through your spirit. Here is further proof in the Word.

Whoever has no rule over his own spirit is like a city broken down, without walls.

Proverbs 25:28

If your walls are broken down and your soulish realm rules over your spirit, you know that you are not rooted and grounded in the Word of God. The enemy will just keep attacking. He'll use situations like your conflicts with friends, family, old relationships, or past experiences to bombard you emotionally until you crumble or until you do something to supplant his attacks against your life.

I know you've read this statement several times already, but I can't emphasize it enough. Knowledge alone is not enough! How many well-known ministers, who have tremendous knowledge of the Word of God, have we read about in the headlines because they fell into sin? Every one of them could quote chapter and verse to you from the Bible all day long, but their souls were out of control. Most of them had become so busy doing things "for" God that they hadn't kept their inner man strengthened by focusing "on" God and lost their intimacy with Him. They were not ruling their spirit man, and the enemy came in and took them down.

STOP, LOOK, & LISTEN

Here's what a guest speaker at a Bible school graduation advised the graduates. He said, "Don't get stopped by the devil on the way to your future. You are a messenger of the Most High God. Just like a railroad crossing says, 'Stop, Look, and Listen,' you must have a stopping time with Jesus every single day. No matter how big your God-given goals are, you must take time to be with Him. You are the only one who can stop you. You can only be successful with God as you spend time with Him. Set your goals and write them down, but don't forget to put in some stopping time with Jesus."

The intensity in the speaker's voice rose as he continued nailing down point after point. "God has a plan...We're all preachers in training...God sent Paul to prison to write thirteen books in the Bible...Joseph went from the pit to prison before he made it to the palace, because God had to get Joseph out of Joseph before he could save his family and his nation, the lineage of Christ...The harder the trial is the more God is in it...God isn't interested in your works, He is interested in you...Don't fall in love with the things of this world, fall in love with Jesus!"[81]

The man who shared this wisdom knew firsthand what happens when a person let's his soul and flesh rule over his spirit. He had experienced the devastation the enemy causes in the life of an anointed man or woman of God who hasn't kept his or her spirit man fed with the implanted Word of God. He also learned that he had to take responsibility for his spirit man because blaming other people for doing him wrong and trying to hide behind all of the emotional baggage from his past was part of what got him in trouble in the first place.

A well-known evangelist lost everything in this world except his children and Jesus. Through the trials and pain of prison life, he learned that God really desires for us to have a soul that prospers, but that in order to experience this godly prosperity, our spirit must be in ascendancy, ruling over our soul and flesh. He learned how critical it is to keep the spirit man strong to be able to wield the shield of faith and quench the fiery darts of the enemy.

LIFT UP THE SHIELD OF FAITH

Have you ever considered how much strength it takes to lift a shield in battle or what a fiery dart really looks like? The pictures we most often see of God's armor do not truly depict the type of shield used by soldiers to deflect flaming arrows. In ancient days, Roman soldiers used two types of shields. One was a small, round shield about 14 inches in diameter. This was used in hand-to-hand combat to deflect swords and knives. The other shield was called a door shield because it resembled a large door made from lightweight wood covered with thick leather. It was large enough for the soldier to crouch behind. Before battle the soldier soaked the shield with water so that when the enemy's arrows that had been soaked in tar and set on fire hit the shield, the fire would be quenched. It also protected the soldier from being splattered with hot tar from the arrow as it hit the shield.[82]

FIGHTING IN UNITY

Soldiers often locked their door shields together in unity as they moved forward on the battlefield. You may have seen this in movies such as *Braveheart*.[83] It shows how important it is to have others fighting alongside us with their shields of faith poised for battle. When you are in a fight for your life, you don't want someone next to you who is an emotional wreck. It won't do you any good to sidle up to each other and cry your eyes out. You have to be prepared to fight in the unity and strength of faith in the Word of God.

YOUR WEAPON IS THE WORD

Now, can you picture yourself lifting a "door shield" to quench the fiery darts the devil sends your way? It takes a lot more strength and preparation to use this shield of faith than you might have realized. I hope you also recognize that the fiery darts spoken of are not like the little plastic darts kids today use for a game of darts. The enemy is firing full-sized arrows covered with flaming black tar meant to kill and maim, and you must be prepared to fight back with the weapons God has provided for you, primarily the Word of God.

> For the word of God is living and powerful, and sharper than any two-edged sword, piercing even to the division of soul and spirit, and of joints and marrow, and is a discerner of the thoughts and intents of the heart.
>
> Hebrews 4:12

Let's also read this verse in the *Amplified* version to gain even greater clarity.

> For the Word that God speaks is alive and full of power [making it active, operative, energizing, and effective]; it is sharper than any two-edged sword, penetrating to the dividing line of the breath of life (soul) and [the immortal] spirit, and of joints and marrow [of the deepest parts of our nature], exposing and sifting and analyzing and judging the very thoughts and purposes of the heart.
>
> Hebrews 4:12 AMP

A CASE OF STOLEN IDENTITY

Ken's mother had died three months ago from cancer, and now he was making funeral arrangements for his father who had died suddenly from a heart attack. In discussing the finances and the estate with his siblings, he discovered a deeply hidden, family secret that shook him to the core. Ken had been adopted as a baby and everyone else in the family knew it but him. He had loved his parents dearly and never had any reason to suspect he wasn't blood relation with his sister and brother. He was devastated.

All sorts of questions began bombarding Ken's mind. Who was he really? Why had this been kept from him? Why had his birth parents rejected him and given him away? He began going back and analyzing events in his childhood and became suspicious of the motives of other family members. Anger rose up in him every time he thought about his adoptive parents. He even found himself putting up walls with his wife and children. He buried his hurt and pain and spent more time at the office, often not coming home until after everyone else was in bed. Then his relationships at work began to unravel and his job was in jeopardy.

Through this difficult time, Ken had been attending church on a regular basis. He heard the Word being preached, but like many others in the church, he wasn't living it the rest of the week. His soul was ruling and the enemy took full advantage. He needed the implanted word of God spoken of by the apostle James.

Therefore lay aside all filthiness and overflow of wickedness, and receive with meekness the implanted word, which is able to save your souls. But be doers of the word, and not hearers only, deceiving yourselves. For if anyone is a hearer of the word and not a doer, he is like a man observing his natural face in a mirror; for he observes himself, goes away, and immediately forgets what kind of man he was. But he who looks into the perfect law of liberty and continues in it, and is not a forgetful hearer but a doer of the work, this one will be blessed in what he does.

James 1:21-25

Ken's emotions were in chaos when he finally cried out to God for help. The enemy had used the death of his loving parents to plant seeds that shook Ken's identity and self-worth. Instead of building himself up and gathering strength from the Lord and from those who loved him, Ken listened to the voices in his head telling him he was an outcast. Anger and suspicion took over and almost destroyed every relationship he had.

THE IMPLANTED WORD BUILDS THE SPIRIT

Only the implanted Word of God was able to build up his spirit and deliver him from the emotional baggage the enemy had thrown at him in a time of weakness. He had to lay aside the bitterness he felt toward his adoptive parents for not telling him about his adoption. When Ken disciplined himself to get back into his personal morning prayer time and Bible study, he began to see issues more clearly. He repented and sought forgiveness from those he had wounded and began to heal in his emotions.

What would happen if someone followed you home from church with a video camera and taped your life for the following week? What emotional baggage would we see on the tape? What roots of bitterness, jealousy, or fear would be evident? How many times did someone push your button and you exploded?

SUBMIT TO THE DELIVERING POWER OF THE WORD

Take a lesson from Ken's experience and submit your life to the delivering power of the Word. It is the only thing that will pierce even to the division of soul and spirit, exposing the root causes of what is making your soul (your mind, will, and emotions) to dominate your spirit. It will allow you to see what clearly needs to be changed in your life. Take the steps the apostle James outlined to get the implanted Word into your spirit. You will be blessed.

Get rid of bitterness, anger, jealousy, and any other wickedness operating in your life.

Receive what the Word has for you with meekness. I want to clarify that meekness is not weakness. Humility is a virtue and it will literally save your soul from destruction.

Be a doer of the Word, not a hearer only.

Let the Word of God be your final authority.

Listen to the voice of the Holy Spirit.

DRAW ON YOUR OWN SPIRITUAL STRENGTH

There is an anointing for the corporate setting of the body of Christ to hear the teaching of the Word, but we must not forsake the time we spend alone with the Lord. Some people spend all their time floating from one meeting to another and are never really directed by the flow of the Holy Spirit. They aren't even living on their own spiritual strength; they are drawing off someone else's. That is a dangerous place to be; because when a time of testing or trial comes, they fall apart. People like this go to every meeting they can and rub elbows with the "Who's Who of Christianity," but when they go home, their family is in chaos. They can't discipline their children, and their emotions are out of control. They don't understand how to battle their emotions with the Word, because they don't have enough of the Word down in their spirit.

Every believer needs to grow and develop in the Word and to be able to discern what is going on in the spiritual realm. The only way to grow in these areas is to spend time in the Word and before God in your own prayer time. Corporate teaching or even family devotions must not be a substitution for private devotions.

VISIT YOUR PRAYER CLOSET DAILY

God has sent the Holy Spirit to teach you in your own prayer closet. It is in this place of intimacy when you get on your knees before God and seek His face that He begins to speak to you and show you the things you need to change in your life. The Holy Spirit will expose areas of weakness in your life where you are being controlled by the flesh rather than by the spirit. He does this not because He wants to punish you, but because He loves you and desires that you walk in the fullness of life that He has already prepared for you!

I have learned to protect and guard my time alone with the Lord. If I know it is going to be a busy day and the rest of the family is going to be up early, then I plan to get up super early. I receive more insight for our church and for my own personal life in my quiet times. It is rare that God speaks to me in the public arena.

GOD SPEAKS IN PRIVATE

Let me share this story about how God has cut things out of my life. I grew up playing soccer and other sports. Being very competitive, I was a rough and emotional player. Believe it or not, I was taught how to break people's legs and how to really injure people (this was before I knew the Lord). I learned quickly that when I was playing ball, I had to stay alert and protect myself. I've had my leg snapped and broken by another player.

I played soccer in Europe, and they really throw you all over the place. I learned a lot of tricks playing there.

When I moved to Hawaii in 1981, I hadn't played soccer for a long time, but I decided a little soccer wouldn't hurt me. Now that I had Jesus in my life, I knew my old behavior and soccer-playing tactics were not right in the sight of God. But, sure enough, in the heat of competition, I sometimes found myself challenging my opponents and reverting to my old dirty tricks to try to gain the advantage over them. Before I knew it, we were battling one another and trying to take each other out, knowing that we could easily injure each other. I was doing exactly what I knew God didn't want me to do.

THE COLUMBIAN DEVIL

One guy from Columbia must have had the devil on him. One day we were playing, and he got me mad. Now, I was saved and somewhat sanctified, but I knew how to get forgiveness later! I took him out, but I didn't take him out good enough because he got back up. Everywhere I went that brother was following me. He had one mission: to take me out.

We got into it again and again. After a while, he just started chasing me all over the field. We weren't even playing soccer anymore. He was trying to play tag you're it; but for him, it was for keeps. The officials finally had to restrain him. I fed off that kind of rough play. I liked to throw elbows and run. When the coach or the ref would say anything, I'd say, "Who, me? I didn't do anything."

I was playing two or three times a week and just eating it up. I didn't always play that rough, but I definitely had an anger problem that seemed to manifest on the field. I thought it was okay because everybody played that way.

THE WRONG KIND OF OFFENSE

At that time, God hadn't spoken to me about being a pastor yet; but I was reading my Bible and preparing myself for the call of God on my life. One day I was reading in the book of Matthew and the Holy Spirit started dealing with me about offenses.

Woe to the world because of offenses! For offenses must come, but woe to that man by whom the offense comes! If your hand or foot causes you to sin, cut it off and cast it from you. It is better for you to enter into life lame or maimed, rather than having two hands or two feet, to be cast into the everlasting fire.

Matthew 18:7,8

As I was reading, the Lord started to deal with me, but I said, "Lord, I'm not going to cut off my hand." Then He went to the foot, and I tried to read past what He was saying. Have you ever done that? God is trying to talk to you. It's like little lights are flashing, and it becomes real clear what God is saying in the passage you are reading; but since you don't want to deal with it, you just keep reading. Then, everything gets real foggy, and you have to go back. The conversation goes something like this:

"Lord, are You trying to tell me something?"

"Yes, I want you to cut off all sports."

"I can't do that." (This was where I tried to negotiate with Him, but He didn't buy it. He came right to the point.)

"If you don't, you're never going to fulfill or step into the next phase of your life."

God said this to me during a private time of Bible study and prayer. I can still see myself in my apartment sitting with my back up against the wall at about 6:15 in the morning. He said, "Cut it off, and cut it off now."

It wasn't easy; but when I was obedient and stopped playing competitive sports, the Lord started opening new doors for me.

The reason I shared this story with you is because sports had been an important part of my life, and I never wanted to admit I had an anger problem.

The Lord said to me, "You've got to bring this thing under control, because it will manifest in other areas of your life." It was during my private times with Him that He began to take me through a process of renewing my mind in the Word. I had to deal with many emotional issues from my past. God spoke, and I listened.

GET PREPARED FOR BATTLE

I cannot overemphasize the importance of having a private devotional time. God wants to talk to you as personally as He did with me if you will give Him the chance. He will lead you, guide you, and help you to build up your inner man, your spirit. His appointment book is open today, and I happen to know you're on His schedule. He is ready to talk with you right now, tonight, and tomorrow morning. Are you? He is ready to prepare you for battle. There's no other way to do it. Are you willing to fight? No one else can do it for you. It's time to press on through whatever is trying to hold you back from fulfilling your destiny.

KNOW YOUR ENEMY

A soldier doesn't go into battle without knowing with whom he is fighting. That was one of the most difficult aspects of the war in Vietnam. The Viet Cong infiltrated the American ranks, as dishwashers, cooks, laundry workers, and other such needed positions. By day, they worked in the U.S. military camps; but at night, they returned from their Viet Cong units to attack and disappear into the darkness. It was frightening for U.S. soldiers to discover a dead Viet Cong was the man who had been cooking their breakfast that morning. Our soldiers had to be on their guard constantly. You should be too.

FOCUS ON THE REAL ENEMY

When you are executing your power as a fighter, you must know who your enemy is. It's not your spouse, your kids, your boss, or your neighbor. It's the devil that is a liar and a deceiver. He uses people and events to distract you and to keep you in turmoil, just as the Viet Cong did with the U.S. soldiers. Therefore, you must keep your focus on the devil, not on those he may be using. The true battle is in the spiritual realm, but the devil tries to get you to fight in the realm of flesh and blood. Again, we must go back to the Word.

> For we do not wrestle against flesh and blood, but against
> principalities, against powers, against the rulers of the
> darkness of this age, against spiritual hosts of wickedness in
> the heavenly places.
>
> Ephesians 6:12

KNOW THE PURPOSE OF YOUR FIGHT

You must know for what you are fighting. The ultimate fight is for what you believe because your beliefs govern the overall affairs of your life. The devil wants you to cast away your confidence in the Word.

> Do not, therefore, fling away your fearless confidence, for it
> carries a great and glorious compensation of reward.
>
> Hebrews 10:35 AMP

The devil doesn't want you to fight the good fight of faith. He would rather see you fight social or political issues or other flesh and blood issues in society. By doing this, he prevents you from having confidence in reaping your rewards.

WHO IS WINNING THE BATTLE?

How many people start off believing for their healing but give up after a while because their healing didn't come? How many people start believing for their finances to turn around because they are tithing and giving offerings; but after a season, they give up and stop tithing and sowing seed? How many people start believing for restoration in their marriages; but after a season passes, they quit? We could go on and on. At some point, they have "cast away their confidence" in the promises of God. They are still Christians, and they will go to heaven; but they will never receive God's promises here on earth. Who won the battle? The devil did.

Have you ever lost your confidence? You go to church and tolerate the pastor's teaching, but it goes in one ear and out the other. After a while, you think you're smarter than God and can do things your way. You don't think the devil has any influence in your arena anyway. You don't believe in that spiritual warfare stuff. You're like I was playing soccer. You're willing to fight with somebody in the flesh, but when the devil says, "Hey, it's not me. I'm not even in your neighborhood," you believe him. You'd better figure out who is winning this battle. I can tell you right now, it's not you. God knows it, and the devil knows it.

DO YOU KNOW THE DEVIL'S M.O.?

Your beliefs govern everything in your life. Satan knows that if you believe what the Bible says about you and if you base your decisions on that belief and act on it, he is in dangerous territory. He knows the power of the Word of God, and his ultimate attack on your life is to get you to release your confidence in the authority and truth of God's Word. He doesn't mind if you tolerate it or even if you listen to it. He says, "Listen all you want. Go to church every time the doors open. It's fine with me. Just don't act on it!" The devil's M.O.—modus operandi (mode of operation or strategy)—is to stop you from believing and acting on the Word of God.

WHOSE REPORT WILL YOU BELIEVE?

The essence of a good fight of faith is based on your decision in regards to what you are going to believe. In what are you going to put your faith? In which realm are you going to give credibility—the seen or the unseen, the natural or the spiritual? Who or what will be the dominating factor in your life? What you can see and touch is the seen, but God reveals His promises in the unseen.

The real fight begins when the unseen and the seen realms come in conflict. In the seen realm, the doctor says, "You have terminal cancer, and you're going to die." In the unseen realm, God's report says, "By the stripes of Jesus you are healed!" Whose report will you believe?

Now you have a fight on your hands. You can continue training and go through all the battle tactics you want. Roll on the ground and get muddy, go under the barbed wire, climb the fence, and whatever else; but when the enemy comes on the battlefield, he's out for the kill. The cancer has jumped on your body and the tumors are everywhere. The doctor says there is nothing he can do. What are you going to do? If you want to live, you are going to have to fight the good fight of faith; believe, and act on what the Word of God says when the natural realm is screaming its evidence at you. All you have left is the Word of God. The fight is on, and it is in the spiritual realm.

> While we do not look at the things which are seen, but at the things which are not seen. For the things which are seen are temporary, but the things which are not seen are eternal.
>
> 2 Corinthians 4:18

We have the promises of God that are eternal, and we have the physical evidence of what appears to be happening in the natural realm. The promises are unseen and the physical evidence is seen. The enemy's voice filters through people in this world saying, "This is my evidence; show me yours. I can show you cancer in your body. I can show you sickness in your liver. I can show you divorce. I can show you poverty. I can show you your empty bank account. I can show you the job you just left, and the woman who doesn't like you, the rejection you just felt. I can show you evidence." All you have on your side is God's Word that says, "I will deliver." Who is winning the battle?

Many of you right now have evidence in the physical realm that is screaming and shouting at you. It's taunting you and intimidating you, saying, "Back up, back up, I have control of your daughter." "Back up, I have control of your finances." "Back up, I have control of your marriage." Are you backing up, or are you standing your ground? Better yet, are you charging forward like young David did when he fought Goliath?

CAPTURE A "FAITH VISION"

To fight the good fight of faith, you must capture a "faith vision" of winning in your spirit. You must see things in your mind's eye before they exist. Faith is what it takes when nothing else makes sense in the natural, when you can't physically reach it or see it. A "faith vision" is what takes your miracle or promise from the unseen into the seen world of reality.

Cheryl Salem was crippled and scarred in a terrible car accident when she was eleven years old. Everyone told her what she couldn't do, but Cheryl had a "faith vision" that she would be totally healed. When the doctors said she would never walk again, God created a new bone in her crushed leg. For over six years, she walked with a limp because one leg was two inches shorter than the other. Then in a Kenneth Hagin meeting when she was 17 years old, God totally healed her leg, and it grew out two inches.

Cheryl also had a "faith vision" that she would be Miss America some day. In 1980 when Cheryl walked the runway in Atlantic City wearing the Miss America crown, her "faith vision" went from the realm of the unseen to the realm of reality for the entire world to see. Cheryl saw the miracle of her healing and saw herself wearing the Miss America crown before anyone else could see it. She kept chipping away at the impossible by exercising her faith until it became possible.[84]

FOUR BATTLEGROUNDS OF FAITH

Military strategists all agree that an army taken by surprise is at an extreme disadvantage. This is true whether the battle is physical or spiritual. It is vital to anticipate where and how the enemy is planning to attack. Satan always attacks your weakest point in an attempt to destroy your faith before you can respond to his attack. When you don't respond in faith, you inevitably respond in the flesh and that never works. We're going to examine four battlegrounds on which the enemy attacks your faith so you will be prepared in advance.

Battleground 1: Your Ears

> So then faith comes by hearing, and hearing by the word of God.
>
> Romans 10:17

You must fight to control what and how you hear. Jesus often spoke of the importance of *hearing*. In the parable of the sower, He spoke of being careful about "what" we hear in Mark 4 and "how" we hear in Luke 8.

> "If anyone has ears to hear, let him hear." Then He said to them, "Take heed what you hear. With the same measure you use it, it will be measured to you; and to you who hear, more will be given."
>
> Mark 4:23,24

> Therefore take heed how you hear. For whoever has, to him more will be given; and whoever does not have, even what he seems to have will be taken from him.
>
> Luke 8:18

Did you know that some people think they are hearing, but they're not? In an earlier chapter, we talked about the art of listening in order to really *hear* the person who is talking. Have you ever let your mind wander when you are hearing a message on a subject you've heard preached before? I can attest to this because I've done it myself. While the message is being given, I'm reworking it into a sermon of my own. I have ears but I'm not hearing what the other person is teaching. We need to put on our "listening" ears whenever the Word of God is being read or taught.

Guard what you allow to go into your ears. Does it edify and build you up, or does it bring fear, strife, unclean thoughts, and confusion? If the enemy can get you to hear more of the world's opinion than the Word of God, you will have more faith in the world than in the Word of God. How much time do you spend listening to the news on TV in comparison to listening to the Word of God? Many people allow the TV or radio to be playing all the time in their homes. Some even go to sleep at night with the TV or radio playing in their bedroom. This is an open door for the enemy to plant all kinds of junk in your mind and spirit.

I'm talking about secular *and* Christian media. There is a lot of distorted doctrine and unbelief coming from both camps, and you need to filter what you allow your ears to hear. Even if you don't think you are listening, your subconscious mind is taking it all in. To have the strength to battle in times of conflict you must fill your ears and mind with the Word of God—the unabridged version. Faith comes by hearing regardless of what you put your ear to hear, so use discernment and discretion.

Here's another thought to consider. What you believe today is really just a product of what you have heard most frequently in the past. If you grew up much like I did being told time and again that you will always be poor because that is the way it is for every Mexican living in America, and you can see the evidence of their words in your life, what are you going to believe? It is going to take more than one promise box of Scripture to deliver you from that mindset. I heard that message and lived it for 23 years. I had to fight to hear a different message from the Bible. I'm the kind of person who releases my faith on the "buts," "ifs" and "whatsoevers" in the Bible. An occasional word on prosperity was not enough to deliver me from insufficiency. I had to plug my ear into the Word on a continual basis to get it through my ear gate and into my heart. You're going to have to do the same by taking these four steps:

1) Attend a strong, Bible-teaching church.

2) Listen to anointed teaching and worship tapes.

3) Read the Bible and other faith-filled books.

4) Speak and confess the Word of God out of your mouth and into your ears.

It will be a fight because there are many distractions in the world shouting for your attention. The average American watches 30 hours of TV a week. Combine that with your workweek, and it doesn't leave much time for the Word. You're going to have to purpose in your heart to shut out these distractions by putting a filter on what you allow your ears to hear and, if necessary, by changing your daily habits.

Battleground 2: Your Mind

And do not be conformed to this world, but be transformed
by the renewing of your mind, that you may prove what is
that good and acceptable and perfect will of God.

Romans 12:2

Renewing your mind is a constant fight of faith. If your
thinking is stinking, it's time to renew it. We've already talked
about this in previous chapters, but it is a key to living a life of
victory rather than defeat.

And don't forget, just because you're saved doesn't mean
your mind has been renewed. In this chapter of Romans, the
apostle Paul was addressing born-again, Spirit-filled, blood-washed
Christians, and they were carnally minded.

Every time an unclean or unrighteous thought comes into
your mind, rebuke it in the name of Jesus. You are the only one
who can guard your thinking. It takes a dogged determination to
do this. Don't get lazy and let it go. It's the little foxes that spoil
the vine, because what we think is what we become and do.

For as he thinketh in his heart so is he.

Proverbs 23:7 KJV

This story reveals what can happen when negative thoughts
are planted in someone's mind.

A man had been selling hot dogs along the side of the road
for a long time. He didn't hear or see well so he didn't listen to
the radio or read the newspaper. His only advertisement was a
sign he put up on the highway telling how good his hot dogs

were. Every day he called out to passers by to buy a hot dog, and they did.

As his business grew, the man increased his meat and bun orders and bought a larger grill to cook more hot dogs. Then his son came home from college and said, "Father, haven't you been listening to the radio or reading the papers? We're in the middle of a recession. The European situation is terrible, the Japanese situation is worse, and the situation here is worst of all."

The old man thought, *Well, my son is in college. He reads the newspapers and listens to the radio. He must know what he's talking about.* So he decreased his meat and bun orders and took down his sign. Sales dropped out of sight.

"You're right," the old man said to his son a few days later. "We certainly are in the midst of a terrible recession."[85]

The enemy often uses other people close to us to plant negative thoughts in our minds. We must guard our minds from our own thoughts and those that come to us from others. It takes mental discipline and effort to control our thoughts. It takes wisdom to know what and to whom we should listen.

Battleground 3: Your Words

Now faith is the substance of things hoped for, the evidence of things not seen. For by it the elders obtained a good testimony. By faith we understand that the worlds were framed by the Word of God, so that the things which are seen were not made of things which are visible.

Hebrews 11:1-3

The words of our mouth have a direct effect on our faith. In other words, get your tongue in line with the Word of God if you want a good report.

We defeat ourselves with our tongue more often than not. Taming our unruly tongue is probably one of the most difficult battles we face. We cannot do it in the natural. It takes the power of the Holy Spirit, the Word of God, and the blood of the Lamb.

Everything that exists in the natural world has a spiritual root. It was not made of things that are visible. The world was made by words of faith spoken by God. We are created in His image, and He has given us the power of attorney we learned about earlier—the name of Jesus. He has given us dominion over this earth; and when we speak words of faith from our hearts, we are framing the world we're going to step into tomorrow.

If you change the spiritual root, you change the fruit. Therefore, if you want to change your circumstances, you are going to have to change the spiritual root from which they spring forth. How can you do this? By putting words of faith in your mouth, you change the temporal world around you. Faith is the change agent, and your words are the containers of that faith.

The devil does everything in his power to rob you of a good confession. He wants you to speak doubt and unbelief, fear and torment, sickness and disease. You don't have to fall into his trap. The fastest way to defeat the devil is to speak the Word of God directly into every situation in your life. He hates to hear you do that, and he won't stick around for long. When the devil is telling you that you won't make the rent payment this month, say, "My God supplies all my needs according to His riches in Christ Jesus."

Remember, believing God that you are prosperous according to His Word is not denial. It's just calling those things that are not as though they are!

Get your thinking and your talking lined up with the Word, and fight the good fight of faith with a positive confession of your mouth. Here are more Scriptures on which to meditate regarding the power your words carry in battle.

> A man will be satisfied with good by the fruit of his mouth.
>
> Proverbs 12:14

> He who speaks truth declares righteousness, but a false witness, deceit. There is one who speaks like the piercings of a sword, but the tongue of the wise promotes health. The truthful lip shall be established forever, but a lying tongue is but for a moment.
>
> Proverbs 12:17-19

> A man shall eat well by the fruit of his mouth, but the soul of the unfaithful feeds on violence. He who guards his mouth preserves his life, but he who opens wide his lips shall have destruction.
>
> Proverbs 13:2,3

> A wholesome tongue is a tree of life, but perverseness in it breaks the spirit.
>
> Proverbs 15:4

BATTLEGROUND 4: YOUR ACTIONS OF FAITH

...faith without works is dead.

> James 2:20

If you don't put action to what you believe, it will all be for nothing. Here is an example. You wake up in the morning with flu symptoms. You have 1 Peter 2:24 engrained in your heart and speak these words, "By Your stripes, Jesus, I am healed of any flu symptoms!" Then you roll over and say, "Honey, call the office and tell them I'm not coming in today. I've got the flu." By your last statement you just annihilated the whole thing. You lost the battle right there.

Your action has to correspond with your words. If you believe you are healed, then pay no attention to those symptoms, get out of bed, and go to work, confirming God's Word until the devil gives up.

I was preaching about Christ, the Healer, one night and the anointing was powerful. All of a sudden, my body started aching with every step I took. My mind was thinking, "You can call somebody up here to take your place. They'll be led by the Spirit with a good message." But my spirit was saying, "No. You've got to walk this thing through. You've got to have corresponding action."

I preached that message through, confessing the Word and praying in the Spirit. We laid hands on the sick, and God moved in a powerful way. When the anointing was on me, I felt the pain lift, but as soon as I stepped off the stage and got into my car, the pain came back. The first thing I did was to pull out a healing tape, put it in the player, and turn it up full volume. I drove home with pain racking my body, confessing the Word of God.

When I got home, the pain was still there. I went to bed and put a tape with Scriptures about giving thanks in the tape player by the bed and started thanking God for my healing. In the morning, still in pain, I rolled out of bed for my prayer time and went to my prayer closet. For two hours I walked the floor praying the Word. My healing hadn't manifested yet, but I was healed. It was about 11:00 A.M. when I realized the pain was gone, and I was fine.

There comes a time when you have to put your faith on the line and prove that Satan is defeated! Satan can only win if you let him. You must begin by having God's Word in you so you can establish proper beliefs. Next, you must renew your mind and your thought life by casting down every imagination that is contrary to the Word of God. Then, speak words of faith that put substance to the hope you confidently expect. Finally, put into action what you believe, think, and say. Satan will fight you on every front, but don't quit. Dig in your heels and execute your power as a fighter to hear, think, speak, and do God's Word. The victory is yours for the taking.

TAKE ACTION TODAY

1) What action do you need to take to enforce the enemy's defeat in your life?

2) When was the last time you had to fight to lay hold of one of God's promises? Who won the battle?

3) In what areas do you need to rule over your spirit? What specific steps will you take to do it?

4) Who will you call upon to stand and fight with you in unity?

5) Write down the action steps you will take in the next 21 days to fight on the four battlegrounds of faith.

Chapter 11

{ Let Go and Let God }

"You can accomplish more in one hour with
God than one lifetime without Him."[86]

A re you inheriting God's promises in all areas of your life?
Are you maximizing your full potential and living a life
of excellence? We all wish we could unequivocally
answer yes to both of these questions. In truth none of us have
arrived there yet, but that should be our goal. Believe it or not,
such a high goal is attainable if we would simply trust God to
reward us according to His Word.

> If you want favor with both God and man, and a reputation
> for good judgment and common sense, then trust the Lord
> completely; don't ever trust yourself. In everything you do,
> put God first, and he will direct you and crown your efforts
> with success.
>
> Don't be conceited, sure of your own wisdom. Instead,
> trust and reverence the Lord, and turn your back on evil;
> when you do that, then you will be given renewed health
> and vitality.
>
> Proverbs 3:4-8 TLB

According to this Scripture we have two choices: to trust God to direct us and reward us, or to be conceited and prideful by trusting in our own wisdom. In this independent, rebellious world in which we live, too often we choose to live out the Frank Sinatra song in which he sings, "I did it my way"![87]

WHAT IS THE EVIDENCE OF YOUR TRUST?

What is your reputation with God? Does He see you trusting Him or trying to do things your way? God knows what is in your heart and whether you truly trust Him or rely on your own resourcefulness to get what you think you need. How often do you even think about God as you go about your day?

The children of Israel saw God miraculously intervene on their behalf as He brought them out of Egypt. Imagine what it must have been like to see the Red Sea part so they could escape from Pharaoh's army. Yet, within days they were complaining about whether God could really provide for their needs. They had been delivered out of Egypt but, obviously, Egypt hadn't been taken out of them.

Jesus said that as believers we are in the world but not of the world. However, we still have much of the spirit of the world in us when we hold on to the things that hinder us from really trusting God. That is when He sees us trusting in ourselves or in other people to get what we want or where we want to be. Do you make things happen for yourself, or do you use good judgment and common sense by being led by the Holy Spirit?

GOD WANTS TO TAKE CARE OF US

When we "let go and let God," we make a conscious decision to stop trusting in our own wisdom to make things happen on our behalf and put our complete trust in God to do it for us. It is His desire to care for us. When we enter into a trusting relationship with God, we realize this awesome benefit. We can retire from "self care" and rest in "His care." Doesn't that sound wonderful? Then why don't we let Him take care of us?

The biggest stumbling block is in not knowing "how" to trust God. It doesn't happen automatically. We have to exercise building our trust in God just as we do in building trust in our natural relationships. Too often, because we have been hurt in our human relationships, we put God on probation to make Him earn our trust.

I have seen this over and over again in counseling sessions. People who have not had loving, nurturing relationships with their earthly fathers find it impossible to have an intimate relationship with their heavenly Father. This is especially true when there has been severe verbal, physical, or sexual abuse. The man who was supposed to love and care for them instead destroyed their innocence and caused indescribable pain. With no experience record to follow, this son or daughter cannot comprehend a father's love. Sometimes they even blame God for what has happened to them. Until the wounded child is able to forgive the parent and allow Jesus to heal the deep emotional and spiritual wounds, there will always be a barrier blocking his or her ability to trust God.

GOD ISN'T LIKE PEOPLE

If you have experienced hurtful relationships and think that taking care of yourself is safer than depending on anyone else to do it, including God, you must realize that God is not like people. He has no failure in Him, and He will never let you down. You can trust Him with all that you are and all that you have. Don't wear yourself out mentally, emotionally, or physically trying to do everything on your own without God's help. He has promised to be there for you.

> Your goodness and unfailing kindness shall be with me all of my life....
>
> Psalm 23:6 TLB

STEP INTO A GOD IDEA

To let go and let God is to step away from a "good idea" and into a "God idea." A "good idea" isn't necessarily bad. It just isn't God's best for us, because our bright ideas are not bright enough. We can follow our own star, but it won't burn as brightly as God's does.

God warns us of the danger of human reason. Higher education has been sought by the socially elite, the wealthy, and the powerful who want to forge their own path. Knowledge has been esteemed as the door that opens the way to social mobility, financial success, and political power. Seeking knowledge is a "good idea," but seeking wisdom is a "God idea." What it really boils down to is that God's ways are not man's ways. God knows the better way.

For My thoughts are not your thoughts, nor are your ways
My ways, says the Lord. For as the heavens are higher than
the earth, so are My ways higher than your ways, and My
thoughts than your thoughts.

Isaiah 55:8,9

DON'T STRADDLE THE FENCE

To receive God's best we must lean our entire personality on
God in Christ and put our complete trust and confidence in His
power, wisdom, and goodness. When we trust in Him, we cannot
lean on our own understanding. We can't straddle the fence and
hold back a part of our heart. God demands *all of us* and *all our
ways* to be submitted to Him if we want to reap the rewards of His
promises. We've read some of these Scriptures already, but I want
to really nail down this understanding in your spirit.

> In order that you may not grow disinterested and become
> [spiritual] sluggards, but imitators, behaving as do those
> who through faith (by their leaning of the entire personality
> on God in Christ in absolute trust and confidence in His
> power, wisdom, and goodness) and by practice of patient
> endurance and waiting are [now] inheriting the promises.
>
> Hebrews 6:12 AMP

> Lean on, trust in, and be confident in the Lord with all your
> heart and mind and do not rely on your own insight or
> understanding. In all your ways know, recognize, and
> acknowledge Him, and He will direct and make straight and
> plain your paths.
>
> Proverbs 3:5,6 AMP

PUT A DEMAND ON GOD

When we make decisions without God's input, we aren't acknowledging Him. However, when we trust in Him with *all* of our heart and mind, He is *obligated* to direct our paths. His Word doesn't lie. God doesn't want you to be misguided and end up with a 50 percent good idea or a relationship that is only good 50 percent of the time. He wants you to live a "zoe" kind of life (the absolute fullness of life) that we talked about in the last chapter.

When God says to trust the Lord with all your heart, He isn't talking about your blood pump. He is talking about your spirit man. God will illuminate your mind, but He speaks to your heart, your inner man, through the Holy Spirit. In order to be "Spirit-led," you must consecrate yourself to God's plan for your life instead of following after a plan of your own making. *The Message Bible* explains this in simple, everyday language.

> Trust God from the bottom of your heart; don't try to figure out everything on your own. Listen for God's voice in everything you do, everywhere you go; He's the one who will keep you on track. Don't assume that you know it all. Run to God! Run from evil! Your body will grow in health and your very bones will vibrate with life!
>
> Proverbs 3:5-8 MESSAGE

TRUST AND OBEY

The question I put to you is this: Do you want to obey God, or do you want to try to figure it out on your own? Don't answer this too quickly. Think about it. When you are arguing with your spouse, sibling, or friend, do you want to obey God and walk in humility, forgiveness, and love, or do you want to put that person in his or her place? We've all been at such a decision point. Our flesh rebels against relying on God. We start looking to our own reason and justifying in our mind why this person deserves to be told or shown what is what.

When the Columbian soccer player was hitting me, my flesh rose up in anger; and I justified why I had the "right" to take him out of the game no matter what the cost. That was when God stepped in for my own good. It was a "God idea" for me to cut off the sports in my life. I had a choice of whether to be obedient or not. If I hadn't chosen to trust in the Lord and lean on His understanding, I might not be pastoring Word of Life Christian Center today. My flesh said, "But I love my sports." I had to listen to and be led by the Holy Spirit onto God's path for my life. I'm blessed today because I trusted God all those years ago.

THE BREATH OF GOD VERSUS
HUMAN UNDERSTANDING

You may be asking, "But how do I know if I am being led by the Holy Spirit?" The Holy Spirit will bear witness with your spirit and illuminate your mind. That is what we call spiritual discernment. The Bible calls it the "breath of God."

> But there is a spirit in man, and the breath of the Almighty gives him understanding.
>
> Job 32:8

We need the "breath of the Almighty" to give us under-standing. Heaven has your name written up there and a plan has been predestined for you. There is a direction, a pathway, for you to go. The Holy Ghost has been sent to earth to lead, guide, and instruct you. Some of us aren't tapping into what He is all about, and He is sitting there saying, "Boy, I really wish they would rely on Me. I could make their path so much smoother."

YOU ARE HIS TEMPLE

God made you with the ability to reason. He expects you to think clearly and use the brain He gave you. He respects who you are and what He has placed inside of you. He wants you to know that you are the temple of the Holy Spirit of the living God (1 Cor. 3:16) and to understand what the Holy Spirit has been sent to do in you and through you.

> For as many as are led by the Spirit of God, these are sons of God. For you did not receive the spirit of bondage again to fear, but you received the Spirit of adoption by whom we cry out, "Abba, Father." The Spirit Himself bears witness with our spirit that we are children of God.
>
> Romans 8:14-16

If you are a son or daughter of God, you have the capability of being led by the Holy Spirit in your daily walk. He does it by bearing witness with your spirit *and* illuminating your mind. A friend shared this story that illustrates what can happen when we don't listen to that still, small voice in our spirit.

After meeting with a business client, she was on a busy four-lane highway and decided to stop off at the office supply store. She had pulled into an exit lane when she heard a voice say, "No, don't go that way." She hesitated and her mind was saying, "You're already in this turning lane. It will be easier to just go the way you intended. You might cause an accident trying to change lanes." She listened with her head instead of her spirit and proceeded to exit off the highway.

The road she took to get to the store wound through a residential area. Her mind was still occupied with the business meeting she had just attended when suddenly she heard a police siren. Looking in her rearview mirror, she was surprised to see a motorcycle policeman motioning her to stop.

The policeman walked up to her window and asked, "Do you know why I stopped you?"

"No, not really."

"You just went through a stop sign. Let me see your license and registration please."

As he proceeded to issue her a ticket for the stop sign violation, my friend was shaking her head. She remembered that this side street was a favorite spot for policemen to sit back out of sight and catch people for rolling through this strangely placed stop sign. However, she knew she was guilty on two counts. One was for not listening to the Holy Spirit when He told her not to take that route, and the other was for allowing her mind to be so preoccupied while she was driving that she didn't see the stop sign.

The ticket cost was $60 for court fees and another $50 and six hours of her time to take a defensive driving class to avoid a higher fine and a mark on her license. There was a price tag attached to not being led by the Spirit even in such a simple thing as a driving route. She was grateful the price had not involved an accident.

PRACTICE LISTENING

We all miss it from time to time. The more you pay attention to the Holy Spirit, the more familiar you become with His voice in order to find direction in your daily walk. The Holy Spirit is interested in every aspect of your life, even your driving route. He will only walk in to the degree you open the door. He will never violate His Word.

You may not realize it, but you hear the voice of the Holy Spirit all the time. He doesn't give lengthy definitions and explanations. Often all He says is, "No!" or "Don't do this." You just have to listen for His promptings.

> But as it is written: "Eye has not seen, nor ear heard, nor have entered into the heart of man the things which God has prepared for those who love Him." But God has revealed them to us through His Spirit. For the Spirit searches all things, yes, the deep things of God. For what man knows the things of a man except the spirit of the man which is in him? Even so no one knows the things of God except the Spirit of God. Now we have received, not the spirit of the world, but the Spirit who is from God, that we might know the things that have been freely given to us by God. These things we also speak, not in words which man's wisdom teaches but which the Holy Spirit teaches, comparing spiritual things with spiritual. But the natural man does not receive the things of the Spirit of God, for they are

foolishness to him; nor can he know them, because they are spiritually discerned.

1 Corinthians 2:9-14

Anyone who leans on human reason alone will miss out on the promptings, the leading, and the direction of God. Such a person will try to make things happen from human reasoning and will get into situations God never intended for him to get into. It might be good, but it won't be God's best.

STOP TRYING TO FIGURE GOD OUT

Too often we let our head interfere with God's plan. We think we can figure God out, or we think we can do it better than He can. Sometimes we get impatient and don't think He is moving quickly enough. There is a lot of truth in this old saying, "If you can figure it out, it's not God!" God's way is never logical in our way of thinking, but His way is always best.

If you want God's ways manifest in your life, you are going to have to get a hold of His thoughts. God doesn't leave you wondering how to do this. He promises to show you how.

I will instruct you and teach you in the way you should go; I will counsel you and watch over you.

Psalm 32:8 NIV

WATCH YOUR ATTITUDE

To allow Him to teach us, we must step back and disengage from what I call the "I-can-do-it-myself attitude." If you have ever raised a child, you have encountered this attitude when the little tyke was learning to feed himself or learning how to put on his own shoes. He exerts his independence and emphatically states, "No. I do it!" Self-sufficiency or independence is a much sought after attainment.

For many of us, the "I-can-do-it-myself attitude" of childhood invades our adult decision-making abilities. It comes out when we say, "I can do this." "I have this under control." We get caught up in the emotions of a relationship and never bother to ask God if it is His idea. We hear a hyper sales pitch from an organization and join up without praying or asking the Lord. It may be a good thing for them, but it isn't necessarily right for you. For someone who has faced painful experiences in life, the "I can pull myself up by my bootstraps and go on from here attitude" can become a dangerous pattern of living. It shuts God out of the picture.

Such independent, self-sufficient attitudes should not be true for a Christian. There is no room in God's kingdom for a "self-made" man or woman. A born-again believer must learn to step back into childlike faith and trust in a Father who knows how best to lead. Don't tie His hands by not having the faith to believe His Holy Spirit has been sent to lead you and to believe that you can hear His voice.

STEPS ORDERED BY GOD

Our "good ideas" are no longer adequate. We need "God ideas" for our lives. The "God ideas" are the steps that have been ordered by the Lord. Too many believers are trying to use human logic and reasoning to explain what only childlike faith can comprehend. We have to let go of our way of doing things, our "good ideas," and really trust in the Holy Spirit to show us His "God ideas."

When Paul Stankard was in school, no one knew much about learning disabilities or what is now called dyslexia. Constantly struggling to overcome his reading difficulties, Paul was labeled as a daydreamer and underachiever. The words on a printed page may have been a jumble, but Paul had an unquench-able thirst for knowledge about the beautiful things in nature. He studied the flowers and bugs he encountered in his nature walks and learned their names and characteristics.

Upon graduating from high school at the bottom of his class, Paul had a "good idea." Since he was good at building things with his hands out of wire and string, he decided perhaps he could train at a vocational school to be a mechanic. Paul's father directed him in a different direction, suggesting that he study glassblowing. Paul's second "good idea" was to become a scientific glassblower.

He loved the hands-on experience as he learned the intrica-cies of glassblowing. The classroom work was still a struggle. The dean suggested he give up, but Paul persevered and eventually graduated. His first job was making laboratory glassware for a petrochemical company. If he had settled for this "good" job, his career would have provided stability and security for his family until retirement.

Paul didn't stop there. He wanted to be more creative and get closer to nature again. He began experimenting by making animal glass knickknacks. Then he was introduced to glass floral paperweights. It became his goal to "encapsulate in glass small moments of God's great glory." Over the years, Paul perfected a method of creating hand blown glass plants and flowers in intricate, colorful detail encapsulated within his glass paperweights. Art collectors and museums around the world purchase his lifelike designs.

A "good idea" to become a scientific glassblower became a "God idea" as Paul's talents blossomed into the success God always had in mind for him. He had to trust God when it came time to quit his secure position with the petrochemical company to venture into his full-time artistic profession. God made a way for him and the rewards have been great. Paul says, "When I hold a glass flower up to the light, I can feel our Creator's light flooding through me."[88]

KNOWING = RELATIONSHIP

True trust in God is based on a personal relationship with Him and a divine encounter. It isn't just knowing *about* God, but knowing Him *intimately* and *trusting* Him completely. God longs for us to trust Him with every part of our lives. The only way we can learn to do this is to become a worshiper of God, not just singing songs at church, but also worshiping Him in everything we do. We must praise Him continually and let our thanks and praise flow from our lips every day, both in good times and bad. We must pray in the spirit and take time to be still and listen to what the Spirit is saying to us. God isn't into one-sided conversations. He knows what we need and He wants to lead and guide us into His best plan. Finally, we must stay in the Word on a daily basis, as reading the Bible feeds our spirit. These are not just religious activities. They are life-giving, trust-building, divine encounters.

IS IT MEMORY OR REVELATION?

If you don't spend time in the Word, you are starving your spirit. In other words, you are working off of memory without any revelation, and that is a dangerous place to be. We can memorize Bible verses by rote; but when we read the Bible, it becomes alive to us. How many times have you read a familiar passage and suddenly had a word or a phrase seem to jump off the page at you? It is like you've never seen it before. That is revelation.

Revelation feeds the spirit. It is the way you connect in the spirit realm with God. God is not a physical being with a flesh nature. God is not a mind made up of intellect and emotions. God is a Spirit, and He connects with us through our spirit. That is how we hear what His Spirit is saying to us and why we miss it when we try to connect with Him through our mind or emotions. Our spirit man or inner man is the eternal part of our person that gives our outer man color and personality.

FEED YOUR SPIRIT

We are disciplined to eat three meals a day in the natural. It is equally important to eat a daily diet of spiritual food to strengthen your spirit man. When you begin magnifying the Lord for His goodness and strength no matter what is going badly in your life that day, He shows up and strengthens your spirit man. When you feed off the revelation of His Word, faith will rise up in you. Your weak flesh will be kicked into motion as your spirit man is fed and strengthened.

David dined upon and was strengthened by the spiritual food of praise and worship, revelation, and prayer. Again and again in the Psalms we read how he was victorious in the physical and spiritual battles of his life as he continually gave all of the glory to the Lord.

> Lord, I trust in you alone. Don't let my enemies defeat me. Rescue me because you are the God who always does what is right. Answer quickly when I cry to you; bend low and hear my whispered plea. Be for me a great Rock of safety from my foes. Yes, you are my Rock and my fortress; honor your name by leading me out of this peril. Pull me from the trap my enemies have set for me. For you alone are strong enough. Into your hand I commit my spirit.
>
> You have rescued me, O God who keeps his promises. I worship only you; how you hate all those who worship idols, those imitation gods. I am radiant with joy because of your mercy, for you have listened to my troubles and have seen the crisis in my soul. You have not handed me over to my enemy, but have given me open ground in which to maneuver.
>
> Psalm 31:1-8 TLB

FIGHTING IN THE SPIRIT REALM

Did you notice that David submitted His spirit to the Lord? David knew he couldn't fight the battle in his own strength. He knew it had to be won in the spiritual realm. He understood what it took to benefit from God's blessings.

But I am trusting you, O Lord. I said, "You alone are my
God; my times are in your hands. Rescue me from those
who hunt me down relentlessly."

Psalm 31:14,15 TLB

Oh, how great is your goodness to those who publicly
declare that you will rescue them. For you have stored up
great blessings for those who trust and reverence you.

Psalm 31:19 TLB

David spoke these words of wisdom to other believers.

Oh, love the Lord, all of you who are his people; for the
Lord protects those who are loyal to him, but harshly pun-
ishes all who haughtily reject him. So cheer up! Take
courage if you are depending on the Lord.

Psalm 31:23,24 TLB

God responds to your praise and adoration, and He
doesn't care whether you have a bad singing voice. He delights
in your prayers and is faithful in fulfilling His Word. He will
take care of you and protect you if you will be less self-reliant
and more God-reliant.

God's plan for your life is not always the easiest path to
follow, but it is always the best because it always leads you to
victory. You may fall in a pothole or stub your toe on a rock along
the path because these things happen in life. He doesn't want you
to give up. His Word says to walk in love, forgive those who
offend or hurt you, and press on in His strength.

WATCH OUT FOR DETOURS

The enemy sometimes uses "good" people and "good" things to distract us and get us off track from a God idea. Beware of such detours. Don't let him get you off track. Keep your spirit fed and listen to the Holy Spirit to discern any danger along the path.

Have you ever watched the Indy 500 race? The cars are racing around the track and suddenly one gets in trouble and several cars get bumped. They go spinning around and around. Some of the cars slide off the track and into the infield. The drivers never even get out of their cars because time is precious, and they don't want to lose the race.

At the speed these cars are moving, a driver uses every ounce of strength and all the knowledge and skill he has to keep his car under control. He is focused on winning the race, and he fights to get back on track as quickly as possible.

A smart driver doesn't let anger flare up at the driver who caused the mishap and climb out of his car screaming, "Look what you made me do. You bumped me. It's your fault. I'm going to get out of this race!" He knows that throwing a pity-party tantrum won't win the race. He focuses on the bigger picture of winning the race, not on the event of the moment.

FOCUS ON THE BIG PICTURE

When circumstances seem out of control, or when others are hurting us or seemingly taking advantage of us, we naturally want to try to line things up in our favor. When we face challenges in life, the easiest thing in the natural, soulish realm is to exit and say, "I don't need this. I'm out of here!" However, we need to understand the big picture and what is really at stake. Jesus trusted His Father to care for Him even when things looked bad for Him. He didn't try to take matters into His own hands and neither should we.

> When He was reviled and insulted, He did not revile or offer insult in return; [when] He was abused and suffered, He made no threats [of vengeance]; but he trusted [Himself and everything] to Him Who judges fairly.
>
> 1 Peter 2:23 AMP

It is difficult to walk in obedience to God and love our fellowman when the primary concern is "Me, Myself, and I." Selfishness means looking out for "Number One" even if it means hurting others or missing windows of opportunity. Trying to take care of ourselves is one of the major causes of strife, wrath, and anger. We must do as the racecar drivers do and focus on the bigger picture of God's plan and purpose and not on the events of the moment that may be disrupting any selfish plans and desires. God has a better way.

TAKE A REALITY CHECK

The enemy looks for your Achilles heel to try to knock you out. He may use a person close to you, an event of the past, difficult circumstances in your present, or an area of weakness in your life to get you to give up and walk away from your calling in God. It is time to take a reality check and face the fact you are in a spiritual battle every day.

To live a righteous life, your flesh is going to scream and your soul is going to say, "I don't want to be here." That is when your spirit man had better be strong and nourished in the Word, in prayer, and in praise and worship.

KEEP THE FIRE IN YOUR EYES

We all have moments in time when we want to lie down and say, "I don't want any more of this." We can't give up. We have to face the enemy of our soul and get back on the track. I love the way the movie *Chariot's of Fire* illustrates this point. Eric Liddell got pushed off the track when he was competing in the 1924 Olympic Games. He got back up with fire in his eyes, threw his head back, and started running. He wasn't going to let anyone keep him from completing what he had started.

PROMISES ARE RELEASED BY FAITH

A multitude of promises in the Word of God are released through faith. No matter what the enemy throws your way, God has made a way for you.

> When the righteous cry for help, the Lord hears, and
> delivers them out of all their distress and troubles.
>
> Psalm 34:17 AMP

In the last chapter, you learned how to execute your power as a fighter on the four battlegrounds of faith: your ears, your mind, your words, and your actions. I am only going to make a couple of additional comments about faith. Paul speaks of the "measure of faith" that is given to every man.

For by the grace given me I say to every one of you: Do not think of yourself more highly than you ought, but rather think of yourself with sober judgment, in accordance with the measure of faith God has given you.

Romans 12:3 NIV

Faith is a gift from God. It grows and develops as we use it. What we do with faith, where we plant it, is up to us. If I choose to put my faith (trust and confidence) in myself, I will soon learn that "self care" does not produce supernatural results. The way to obtain supernatural results is to "let go and let God."

RETIRE FROM "SELF-CARE"

God is a gentleman, and He will not step into your life without being invited to do so. If you aren't willing to cast your cares on Him, His hands are tied. When you stop trying to take care of yourself, you release God to take care of you. God's provisions are available all the time; it is up to us to retire from "self care" and enjoy "His care."

It is comforting to be assured of God's special care no matter what is going on around us. He knows the big picture and the future outcome. He says, "Let go, and let Me handle it."

Casting the whole of your care [all your anxieties, all your worries, all your concerns, once and for all] on Him, for He cares for you affectionately and cares about watchfully.

1 Peter 5:7 AMP

HOW DO YOU REAP HIS REWARDS?

Repeatedly, God's Word teaches us that God is our Defender, our Vindicator, our Strengthener, and our Rewarder. The story of Abram (before God renamed him Abraham) and Lot written in Genesis 13 is one example that proved this to be true.

Abram came out of Egypt and into the land of Canaan. His nephew, Lot, was with him. Both of them had large animal herds, and there wasn't room for them to graze in one place. Their herdsmen were squabbling amongst themselves. Abram did not want any strife between them so he told Lot to choose where he wanted to dwell. Then Abram took what was left.

Lot looked with his natural eyes at the plain of Jordan and saw lush, well-watered land. He tried to take care of himself by choosing what he thought was the best land. He didn't inquire of the Lord and trusted in his own judgment. Lot took his family and herds and journeyed to the east. However, the people from the land that Lot chose were exceedingly wicked. Because of his selfish choice, Lot experienced total devastation when God destroyed the cities of Sodom and Gomorrah.

GOD BROUGHT JUSTICE

Abram trusted in God and God rewarded him. Lot had tried to take advantage of Abram, but God brought justice. Abram received the land of Canaan as an inheritance for his promised descendants who would number so many they couldn't be counted. He received more land than he had before he and Lot split up, and Abram's wealth multiplied greatly.

Lot's demise and Abram's reward illustrate the difference between trying to take care of ourselves and trusting God. Our enemies are powerful against us. We actually give them power over us through lack of faith in God.

THREE PROMISES FOR A BELIEVER

For a believer who calls upon God, there are three distinct promises.

> He will call upon me, and I will answer him; I will be with
> him in trouble, I will deliver him and honor him.
>
> Psalm 91:15 NIV

God promises to be with us in trouble, to deliver us, and to honor us. When God honors a believer, He lifts him up, or elevates him.

> The Lord is my light and my salvation—whom shall I fear?
> The Lord is the stronghold of my life—of whom shall I be
> afraid? When evil men advance against me to devour my
> flesh, when my enemies and my foes attack me, they will
> stumble and fall. Though an army besiege me, my heart will
> not fear; though war break out against me, even then will I
> be confident.
>
> One thing I ask of the Lord, this is what I seek: that I may
> dwell in the house of the Lord all the days of my life, to gaze
> upon the beauty of the Lord and to seek him in his temple.
> For in the day of trouble he will keep me safe in his
> dwelling; he will hide me in the shelter of his tabernacle and
> set me high upon a rock.
>
> Psalm 27:1-5 NIV

THE KEY TO HONOR IS HUMILITY

Therefore, humble yourselves [demote, lower yourselves in your own estimation] under the mighty hand of God, that in due time He may exalt you.

1 Peter 5:6 AMP

Abram's humility was shown when he deferred first choice of the land to Lot. Abram was the leader and had every right to tell Lot where he could settle. Instead, Abram took great care to politely ask Lot to choose.

GET IN LINE FOR PROMOTION

When you humbly defer your care into God's hands, your act of faith places you in direct line for God's exaltation or promotion. In the world's system, you *work hard* and *get* your reward. In God's system, you *trust deeply* and *receive* your reward. God will honor and reward you as you place your trust in Him.

Living by the armor of the flesh invites strife to develop within oneself, with God, and with others. When you are faced with someone who doesn't treat you fairly, humble yourself and simply pray for them. Then trust God to take care of you.

Sandy had worked at the Sanders' Company for over thirteen years. The CEO with whom she had worked closely all those years had recently retired. The transition to new leadership was difficult at times. Sandy took on many additional responsibilities with her already heavy workload, which she performed willingly. Her new boss was demanding and had a quick temper that often flared unexpectedly and without reason. After one particularly difficult meeting, Sandy returned to her office in tears.

As she sat down at her desk, she noticed her Bible was open to Romans 12. Her eyes focused in on these verses:

> Be kindly affectioned one to another with brotherly love; in honour preferring one another; Not slothful in business; fervent in spirit; serving the Lord; Rejoicing in hope; patient in tribulation; continuing instant in prayer.
>
> Romans 12:10-12

Sandy knew what she had to do. From that day forward she prayed blessings on her new boss and asked the Lord's favor to be upon their relationship. She noticed a change gradually taking place over the coming months. Her boss was more respectful and showed confidence in her ideas and work.

A year later when Sandy resigned from her position to move to another state, she was shocked to see tears in her boss's eyes. She had humbled herself and prayed, and God took care of the rest. Trusting God leads to peace!

> But when you pray, go into your [most] private room, and closing the door, pray to your Father, Who is in secret; and your Father, Who sees in secret, will reward you in the open.
>
> Matthew 6:6 AMP

LIVE BY DESIGN, NOT BY DEFAULT

God created you in His image to fulfill His purpose on this earth and throughout eternity. He knew you before you were even formed in your mother's womb, and He already had a plan for you before the seed was planted for your birth. He has made a way for you to fulfill your destiny. He wants you to live by His design, not by your own default.

Many of us have heard this Scripture many times, but not everyone comprehends how awesome a promise it really is. Read it again and again until you have truly planted it in your heart—in your spirit. Hear what God is saying to you. Consecrate yourself to God's plan and stop trying to follow a plan of your own making.

> For I know the thoughts that I think toward you, saith the Lord, thoughts of peace, and not of evil, to give you an expected end. Then shall ye call upon me, and ye shall go and pray unto me, and I will hearken unto you. And ye shall seek me, and find me, when ye shall search for me with all your heart.
>
> Jeremiah 29:11-13 KJV

Notice this version is translated, "to give you an expected end." That confirms God has prepared a way for you in advance. He wants you to *expect* a prosperous and peaceful future.

As with every promise, action is required on your part. To appropriate the promise, you must "call upon Him and pray." That means you must invite Him to step into your life and circumstances, setting aside your own agenda. In other words, get in your prayer closet and invite Him into your presence. Let your petitions and prayers go up to Him to fill the bowls of incense at His altar. Finally, He says to "seek and search for Me with all of your heart." He wants the *real* you, your spirit man, to connect with His Spirit. Seeking and searching requires considerable effort, but once you commit to it, you *will* find Him. Through worship you will come to *know* Him intimately as a son or daughter is meant to know the Father.

God knows the beginning from the end of the big picture in eternity. It is beyond our natural mind to be able to comprehend eternity. All we can do is take one step at a time, one day at a time, and leave the rest in His hands. Hudson Taylor, thought by many to be the "father" of missionary work as we know it today, once said, "God's work done in God's way will not lack God's supply."[89] All it takes is faith and trust in the Creator of the Universe, the Alpha and the Omega, the Lord God Almighty. To maximize your potential and fulfill your God-given destiny, consecrate yourself to be an obedient, willing vessel for His plan and "let go and let God! He will do the rest."[90]

TAKE ACTION TODAY

1) What evidence is there in your life that you trust God and do things His way?

2) On a scale of 1 to 10 with 10 being complete trust, how would you measure your trust level with God?

3) What steps do you plan to take to exercise building that trust level?

4) What pain or old wounds need to be forgiven and released to Jesus for healing?

5) What "good ideas" will you lay aside to focus on a "God idea?"

Conclusion

"Each of us will one day be judged by our standard of life, not by our standard of living; by our measure of giving, not by our measure of wealth; by our simple goodness, not by our seeming greatness."[91]

William Arthur Ward

One of the few men I know who can be measured by his standard of life, by his measure of giving, and by his simple goodness is Charlie Wedemeyer. Twenty-two years ago, Charlie's life was about winning football games as he coached the Los Gatos Wildcats to California's Central Coast Championship. Today, Charlie's life is about winning the battle of life over death one more day. But more than that, it is about what Charlie and his beautiful wife, Lucy, can give to others who are struggling with ALS—Lou Gehrig's disease—or some other difficulty in life. Charlie and Lucy give real meaning to what it means to live *in Christ*. Charlie says, "I live to give others hope."[92]

Charlie has shattered the glass ceiling that says ALS patients have no quality of life once their bodies have been ravaged by the disease. He is determined to live his life on purpose, despite what the doctors say. His fighting spirit, outrageous sense of humor, and unshakeable faith in God have defied the odds of medical science. In 1977 when he was diagnosed with the disease, the doctors gave him one year to live. Charlie went on to coach seven more years of high school football from his golf cart on the sidelines and with Lucy interpreting his coaching instructions by reading his lips.

More than twenty-three years later, Charlie and Lucy still travel all over the country encouraging others to celebrate life no matter what obstacles they may be facing. Traveling is a barrier most would call impossible, but they press on with an entourage of medical assistants, equipment, and a determination to make a difference in the lives of others. Their living testimony defeats society's arguments for right-to-die and assisted suicide legislation.

Charlie was born in Hawaii and grew up in Kalihi Valley. He was the youngest of nine children and learned the value of a loving, loyal family from his parents and siblings. He was a star football player at Honolulu's Punahou Academy where he met a beautiful, blond cheerleader and fell in love. Lucy is still his cheer-leader as well as his hands, his feet, and his voice. Recently Charlie and Lucy blessed us with a visit to Word of Life Christian Center. The disease has weakened Charlie's physical body, but His spirit man soars to heights most of us cannot even imagine. Jesus shines out of his eyes and radiates from his smile. Laughter is definitely good medicine, and the Wedemeyer's administered a big dose to us that day. However, beyond the humor, we were encouraged and challenged to make every second in life count for something, to never take anything for granted, and to press on *through* every trial in life with Jesus at the helm of our vessel.

God's destiny for Charlie Wedemeyer was much different than he imagined it would be. He thought his life was football and coaching, but God had a much deeper walk for him. God was preparing Charlie to be a coach in the game of life for others to see His glory shine out of a willing vessel of unconditional love. What an awesome example His life is for others.

Each of us is at a different level in our walk with God, and each of us has significance and value in God's sight. As the body of Christ, we should not be competing with one another but rather encouraging one another, appreciating our differences, and always having a holy respect for where each one of us is in our personal walk with the Lord. One is not greater than another. We are simply unique in our calling and in our season in life. None of us has fully attained all that God has promised us, but we should be stretching and reaching forward and upward toward Him.

As we proceed along this highway called life, our dwelling place must be the Word of God so that our steps are ordered and directed by Him and our thirst for revelation and righteousness is quenched as Jesus promised.

> Blessed are those who hunger and thirst for righteousness,
> for they shall be filled.
>
> Matthew 5:6

His Word will fill every dry, parched area of your life if you will drink from His well. God wants you to live your life on purpose so that you will reach your destiny in Him. So don't let anything hold you back from moving to the next level He has for you. As you press toward your high calling and are filled with His goodness, His Living Word will change you.

Jesus said we are not to worry about tomorrow, but He didn't say not to plan for tomorrow. He has a destiny for you to fulfill and a plan for you to carry it out. He is taking you ever upward, one level at a time. As you apply the principles in this book and allow the Holy Spirit to lead you, my prayer is that you will discover your destiny and press through every obstacle that may be holding you back.

Don't be content with where you are. Keep reaching forward to those things that are ahead as the apostle Paul did.

> Yes indeed I also count all things loss for the excellence of the knowledge of Christ Jesus my Lord, for whom I have suffered the loss of all things, and count them as rubbish, that I may gain Christ and be found in Him, not having my own righteousness which is from the law, but that which is through faith in Christ, the righteousness which is from God by faith....
>
> Not that I have already attained, or am already perfected; but I press on, that I may lay hold of that for which Christ Jesus has also laid hold of me.
>
> Philippians 3:8,9,12

All that God has for you to achieve is out there waiting for you to make the effort to attain it. It won't come to you automatically; you must press forward and fight for it.

When Kuna and I decided we needed to strengthen our physical bodies so we could walk in health and fitness, we had to press forward and work hard at it. We worked with a personal trainer and soon discovered it wasn't easy pursuing our goals. We had to push ourselves to keep working at it, and we had to learn how to do it correctly. Our trainer had to teach us how to lift weights the right way to get the maximum benefit and not damage our muscles. With time and instruction, we became more skilled and confident in our training and began to reap the benefits as we focused our energy correctly.

It was the same when we started the church. Once we accepted the call to be pastors, we started with small beginnings. Over time, it took persistence and hard work to keep pressing in with prayer and faith to get to where we are today.

The principles and examples I have shared with you in this book are tools to help you focus your energy on what God has for you to accomplish. As you allow the Holy Spirit to lead you, the eyes of your understanding will be opened and His vision for you will be revealed. Take the vision He shows you and bathe it in prayer. As you faithfully apply the principles you have learned, you will find yourself moving from where you are to where you want to be. God has something better ahead for you if your future is centered on Christ and His Word. Press on and execute your power as a fighter in the spiritual realm. Fight the good fight of faith and lay hold of everything God has for you, because His best is yet to come!

As you continue in pressing onward and upward, "may the Lord direct your hearts into the love of God and into the patience of Christ" (2 Thess. 3:5); and may you never be the same again as you follow the path and run the race God has for you.

Endnotes

1 Rosten, *Passion and Prejudice*.

2 *Webster's New World College Dictionary*, p. 1344.

3 Maxwell, *It's Just a Thought...*, p. 42.

4 Maxwell, *Developing the Leader Within*, p. 139-140.

5 Kallestad, p. 24-25.

6 Ibid, p. 28.

7 Ibid, p. 29.

8 *Don't Wait for Your Ship to Come In*, p. 68.

9 Maxwell, *Developing the Leader Within*, p. 140-141.

10 Ibid, p. 141.

11 Ibid, p. 143.

12 Ziglar, *See You at the Top*, p. 205-206.

13 Yancey, *Where Is God When It Hurts?*, p. 198.

14 Baerg, p. 120.

15 Maxwell, *The Winning Attitude*, Introduction.

16 Riley, p. 139.

17 Maxwell, *The Winning Attitude*, p. 13-14.

18 *Lance Armstrong: Champion Cyclist Beats Testicular Cancer*, abcnews.com article, February 16, 1999.

19 Maxwell and Dornan, p. 52.

20 Swindoll, p. 511.

21 Bartleby.com, *Simpson's Contemporary Quotations*, www.bartleby.com/63/76/4876.html.

22 Treat, p. 166-168.

23 *New International Version Bible*.

24 Swindoll, p. 102.

25 Ibid, p. 99.

26 Booher, p. 190.

27 Swindoll, p. 102-103.

28 Evans, *Marriage on the Rock*, p. 213.

29 Swindoll, p. 99.

30 *Effective Business Presentations Seminar Manual*, Section 1.

[31] Andrews.

[32] *Effective Business Presentations Seminar Manual,* Section 1.

[33] Ibid.

[34] Ziglar, *Courtship After Marriage,* p. 113.

[35] Ziglar, *Something to Smile About,* p. 3.

[36] Strong, #3618, p. 51.

[37] *Webster's Ninth New Collegiate Dictionary,* p. 429.

[38] Maxwell, *Developing the Leader Within,* p. 28.

[39] Maxwell, *Leadership 101, What Every Leader Needs to Know,* p. 31.

[40] Maxwell, *Developing the Leader Within,* p. 31.

[41] *Don't Wait for Your Ship to Come In,* p. 71.

[42] www.edcolelibrary.com/lounge/coleisms.

[43] Baerg, p. 182.

[44] Thayer and Smith, *The* KJV *New Testament Greek Lexicon,* "Greek Lexicon entry for Homilia," available from <http://www.biblestudytools.net/Lexicons/Greek/grk.cgi?number=36 57&version=KJV>.

[45] Evans, *Child of Promise,* Chapter 9, p. 16.

[46] Ibid.

[47] Ibid.

[48] Murdock, p. 64.

[49] Maxwell, *Devloping the Leader Around You,* p. 3.

[50] Baerg, p. 182.

[51] Ziglar, *See You at the Top,* p. 206.

[52] Monroe, Preface.

[53] Bacrg, p. 39-40.

[54] Ibid.

[55] Ibid, p. 15-16.

[56] *Don't Wait for Your Ship to Come In,* p. 140.

[57] *The Forbes Book of Business Quotations,* p. 224.

[58] *How to Be an Up Person in a Down World,* p. 19.

[59] *The Forbes Book of Business Quotations,* p. 747.

[60] Crouch, p. 153.

[61] Ibid. p. 163.

[62] Ibid, p. 147.

[63] Bennis, *On Becoming a Leader*, p. 141.

[64] Baerg, p. 137

[65] Maxwell, *Leadership 101*, p. 30.

[66] Maxwell, *The Winning Attitude*, p. 103-104.

[67] *Don't Wait for Your Ship to Come In*, p. 139.

[68] http://www.m-w.com. s.v. "indifference."

[69] Maxwell, *It's Just a Thought...*, p. 126.

[70] Vine, *Vine's Complete Expository Dictionary*, p. 510.

[71] Crouch, p. 37.

[72] www.nhu.edu/studentresoures/leadletter/leadlet2.html.

[73] Maxwell, *It's Just a Thought...*, p. 5.

[74] Covey, p. 46.

[75] Ibid, p. 46

[76] Maxwell, *It's Just a Thought...*, p. 85.

[77] Ziglar, *See You at the Top*, p. 187.

[78] *The Forbes Book of Business Quotations*, p. 25.

[79] Thoene, p. 453.

[80] Vine, *Vine's Complete Expository Dictionary*, p. 367.

[81] Storey, p. 236.

[82] Malone, p. 51.

[83] Mel Gibson, director and producer, *Braveheart* (Paramount Pictures, 1995).

[84] Salem, *A Bright Shining Place.*

[85] Crouch, p. 119.

[86] *God's Little Instruction Book.*

[87] Paul Anka and Frank Sinatra, My Way, 1969.

[88] Stankard, p. 21.

[89] Taylor, "Missions, slogans and quotes from missionaries" available from <http://home.snu.edu/~hculbert.fs/slogans.htm>.

[90] Shibley, p. 112.

[91] Ziglar, *Something to Smile About*, p. 189

[92] Wedemeyer, *Charlie's Victory*, book jacket copy.

References

Andrews, Lindon. "TV Addiction Passes from Parent to Child," *The Dallas Morning News,* October 11, 1999.

Baerg, Kevin. *Created for Excellence* (Tacoma, WA: Inspiration Ministries, 1996), p. 190.

Bennis, Warren. *On Becoming a Leader* (Cambridge, MA: Perseus Publishing, 2003), p. 141.

Booher, Dianna. *The Worth of a Woman's Words* (Nashville, TN: Word Publishing, 1999), p. 190.

Covey, Stephen R. *The 7 Habits of Highly Effective People* (New York, New York: Simon & Schuster, 1989).

Crouch, Van. *Winning 101* (Tulsa, OK: Honor Books, 1998).

Evans, Jimmy. *Child of Promise* (Amarillo, TX: Majestic Media, 1999).

Evans, Jimmy. *Marriage on the Rock* (Amarillo, TX: Majestic Media, 1994).

Effective Business Presentations Seminar Manual, Zig Ziglar Corporation.

God's Little Instruction Book (Tulsa, OK: Honor Books, 1993).

How to Be an Up Person in a Down World (Tulsa, OK: Honor Books, 1994).

Malone, Henry. *Shadow Boxing* (Dallas, TX: Trophy Publishing, 1999).

Mason, John. *Don't Wait for Your Ship to Come In...* (Tulsa, OK: Honor Books, Inc. 1994).

Maxwell, John C. *Developing the Leaders Around You* (Nashville, TN: Thomas Nelson, Inc., Publishers, 1995).

Maxwell, John C. *Developing the Leader Within* (Nashville, TN: Thomas Nelson, Inc., Publishers, 1993).

Maxwell, John C. *Leadership 101* (Tulsa, OK: Honor Books, 1994).

Maxwell, John C. *The Winning Attitude* (Nashville, TN: Thomas Nelson Publishers, Inc., 1993).

Maxwell, John C. *Becoming a Person of Influence* (Nashville, TN: Thomas Nelson, Inc. Publishing, 1997).

Monroe, Myles. *Understanding Your Potential* (Shippensburg, PA: Destiny Image Publishers, 1991).

Murdock, Mike. *The Making of a Champion* (Tulsa, OK: Honor Books, 1995).

Riley, Pat. *The Winner Within* (New York, New York: The Berkley Publishing Group, 1993).

Rosten, Leo Calvin. *Passions and Prejudices: Or, Some of My Best Friends Are People* (New York: McGraw-Hill, 1978).

Salem, Cheryl. *A Bright Shining Place* (Tulsa, OK: Eagle Run Publishing, 1981).

Shibley, David. *Heaven's Heroes* (Green Forest, AR: New Leaf Press, 1994).

Stankard, Paul. "Blossoming in the Light" (Carmel, NY: Guidepost, November, 1999).

Storey, Tim. *It's Time for Your Comeback* (Tulsa, OK: Harrison House, Inc., 1998).

Strong, James. *Strong's Exhaustive Concordance of the Bible,* "Greek Dictionary of the New Testament" (Nashville: TN, Thomas Nelson Publishers, 1990).

Swindoll, Charles R. *The Tale of the Tardy Ox Cart* (Nashville, TN: Word Publishing, 1998).

The Forbes Book of Business Quotations (New York, NY: Black Dog & Leventhal Publishers, Inc., 1997).

Thoene, Brock & Bodie. *The Twilight of Courage* (Nashville, TN: Thomas Nelson Publishers, 1994).

Treat, Casey. *Complete Confidence: The Attitude for Success* (Seattle, WA: Casey Treat Ministries, 1985).

Vine, W.E., *Vine's Complete Expository Dictionary* (Nashville, TN: Thomas Nelson Publishing, 1984).

Webster's New World College Dictionary, Third Edition, (New York, NY: Simon & Schuster, Inc., 1996).

Webster's Ninth New Collegiate Dictionary (Springfield, Massachusetts: Merriam-Webster Inc., 1986).

Wedemeyer, Charlie and Lucy. *Charlie's Victory* (Grand Rapids, MI: Zondervan Publishing House, 1993).

Ziglar, Zig. *Courtship After Marriage* (Nashville, TN: Oliver Nelson, 1990).

Ziglar, Zig. *See You at the Top* (Gretna, Louisiana: Pelican Publishing Company, 1977).

Ziglar, Zig. *Something to Smile About* (Nashville, TN: Thomas Nelson, Inc., 1997).

Prayer of Salvation

God loves you—no matter who you are, no matter what your past. God loves you so much that He gave His one and only begotten Son for you. The Bible tells us that "...whoever believes in him shall not perish but have eternal life" (John 3:16 NIV). Jesus laid down His life and rose again so that we could spend eternity with Him in heaven and experience His absolute best on earth. If you would like to receive Jesus into your life, say the following prayer out loud and mean it from your heart.

Heavenly Father, I come to You admitting that I am a sinner. Right now, I choose to turn away from sin, and I ask You to cleanse me of all unrighteousness. I believe that Your Son, Jesus, died on the cross to take away my sins. I also believe that He rose again from the dead so that I might be forgiven of my sins and made righteous through faith in Him. I call upon the name of Jesus Christ to be the Savior and Lord of my life. Jesus, I choose to follow You and ask that You fill me with the power of the Holy Spirit. I declare that right now I am a child of God. I am free from sin and full of the righteousness of God. I am saved in Jesus' name. Amen.

If you prayed this prayer to receive Jesus Christ as your Savior for the first time, please contact us on the Web at **www.harrisonhouse.com** to receive a free book.

Or you may write to us at:
Harrison House
P.O. Box 35035
Tulsa, Oklahoma 74153

About the Author

Art Sepúlveda, senior pastor of Word of Life Christian Center, is a man of vision, purpose, and passion who desires to make a difference in the State of Hawaii, the nation, and the world. Together with his wife, Kuna, they established Word of Life Christian Center on September 23, 1984, in Honolulu, Hawaii.

> Do all things without complaining and disputing that you may become blameless and harmless children of God without fault in the midst of a crooked and perverse generation, among whom you shine as lights in the world, holding fast the *word of life*....
>
> Philippians 2:14-16

This mandate, to reach people at all levels of society without regard to culture or condition and bring them God's message of hope, has become Pastor Art's passion and lifelong pursuit.

Over the past 20 years, Word of Life Christian Center has grown from 25 to well over 5,000 people attending weekly celebration services. The church also reaches over 2,000 people each week in more than 700 home cell groups called Life Groups dedicated to winning souls, building and nurturing lasting relationships, and making disciples throughout Hawaii.

Word of Life Christian Center is training and educating students of excellence from preschool through high school at Word of Life Academy. The School of Music, Media, and Performing Arts equips students with the skills they'll need to set the pace in today's multimedia driven society.

Pastor Art is reaching people and touching lives through his daily television program—which extends to the nations of the Pacific Rim, Asia, and beyond—annual conferences, outreaches, and guest speaking engagements. Through creative arts and multimedia, his unique style of expressing the Gospel message in relevant and innovative ways continues to impact millions.

Pastor Art lives in Honolulu, Hawaii, with his wife, Kuna, and four daughters, Ashley, Nicole, Alexis, and Natalie.

To contact Pastor Art Sepúlveda
please write to:

Art Sepúlveda
Word of Life Christian Center
550 Queen Street
Honolulu, HI 96813
(808) 528-4044
www.wordoflifehawaii.com

Please include your prayer requests
and comments when you write.

www.harrisonhouse.com

Fast. Easy. Convenient!

- ◆ New Book Information
- ◆ Look Inside the Book
- ◆ Press Releases
- ◆ Bestsellers

- ◆ Free E-News
- ◆ Author Biographies
- ◆ Upcoming Books
- ◆ Share Your Testimony

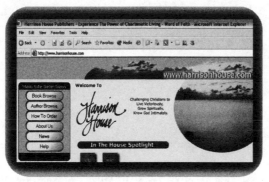

For the latest in book news and author information, please visit us on the Web at www.harrisonhouse.com. Get up-to-date pictures and details on all our powerful and life-changing products. Sign up for our e-mail newsletter, *Friends of the House,* and receive free monthly information on our authors and products including testimonials, author announcements, and more!

Harrison House—
Books That Bring Hope, Books That Bring Change

The Harrison House Vision

Proclaiming the truth and the power

Of the Gospel of Jesus Christ

With excellence;

Challenging Christians to

Live victoriously,

Grow spiritually,

Know God intimately.